PIUS XI: APOSTLE OF PEACE

THE MACMILLAN COMPANY
NEW YORK · BOSTON · CHICAGO · DALLAS
ATLANTA · SAN FRANCISCO

MACMILLAN & CO., Limited
LONDON · BOMBAY · CALCUTTA
MELBOURNE

THE MACMILLAN COMPANY
OF CANADA, Limited
TORONTO

PIUS XI

PIUS XI

Apostle of Peace

BY

LILLIAN BROWNE-OLF

NEW YORK

THE MACMILLAN COMPANY

1938

𝔑𝔦𝔥𝔦𝔩 𝔬𝔟𝔰𝔱𝔞𝔱
ARTHUR J. SCANLAN, S.T.D.
Censor Librorum.

𝔍𝔪𝔭𝔯𝔦𝔪𝔞𝔱𝔲𝔯
PATRICK CARDINAL HAYES
Archbishop, New York.

NEW YORK, February 9, 1938.

38-9244

PRINTED IN THE UNITED STATES OF AMERICA
BY J. J. LITTLE AND IVES COMPANY, NEW YORK

TO GEORGE CARDINAL MUNDELEIN

PRINCE OF THE CHURCH

AND

AMBASSADOR OF CHRIST

NOTABLE CIVIC LEADER

ADMIRABLE ADMINISTRATOR

ENDURING BUILDER

AND

CHAMPION OF PEACE

"I thank God that he made me live in the present day, in the midst of a crisis so universal, so profound and unique in the history of the Church. A man may justly be proud to be a witness, and up to a certain point, an active witness of this sublime drama in which good and evil are joined in one gigantic struggle. No one, at this present hour, has a right to take refuge in mediocrity, and I am certain that from this formidable upheaval the Church will arise more resplendent and better adapted to the necessities of the actual hour."

Pius XI

ACKNOWLEDGMENT

The author wishes to express her indebtedness to the Rev. Angelo Novelli, whose scholarly work PIO XI, Casa Editrice, "Pro Familia," Milano, furnished source material for Chapter V, and to Orazio M. Premoli, Barnabite, whose CONTEMPORARY CHURCH HISTORY (1900-1925) Burns Oates & Washburne, London, has been of invaluable assistance in the creation of the present volume. Other books consulted are duly listed in the Bibliography.

FOREWORD

BEFORE the altar of Saint Peter the stranger in Rome may envision two thousand years of fateful history for Europe and the world. From the tiny group of simple unlettered fishermen who heeded the mandate "Thou art Peter, upon this rock I will build my Church," to the present day when four hundred million adherents acknowledge that audacious claim, the thoughtful stranger sees passing before his mind's eye a vast army of devoted soldiers penetrating the wilderness of the Americas, the wilds of Africa, China and India, the antipodes and the hot sands of the desert. No region has proven too remote, no danger too hazardous, no tribes of men too hostile, to daunt the ardor of these missionaries of the Lord. War, disease, pestilence, famine, death have been their portion. Their depleted ranks have always been refilled. Defeat has never been final.

Powerful monarchs have submitted to the authority of the acknowledged head of Christendom. In the end the Church has always triumphed. "The Church has seen many governments rise and fall," a Dominican monk in San Clemente's once said to me with an inscrutable smile in answer to my indiscreet query.

What is the secret of this power which even her enemies envy? What of the visible head, the Pontiff of Rome? What is the cohesive force behind the Papacy which has made the chair of St. Peter so time-defying? Is it, as her critics affirm, due solely to her uncanny faculty of diplomatic strategy? Does the subtlety of her hierarchy account for the sustained vitality of this unique institution, international in scope—or more properly *super*-national—which puts to shame the petty pretensions of temporal rulers? How explain the phemomenon of the Vatican? Must we concede that the Church derives her stability, not from men, but from a higher power?

This is no casual claim to be lightly thrust aside. In the midst of industrial and social chaos there exists this mighty organization at whose head sits a remarkable man, a man thoroughly convinced that he, through Christ, points the way of life. Amid the turmoil of class jealousies and the frenzied arming of nations sits the representative of a spiritual power who calls upon mankind to put aside their weapons of warfare, who pleads to all the world for an end of strife, who dares to call the wicked by their right names. Like St. John Baptist he cries in the modern wilderness "Repent! Repent!"

The two great modern problems that must be solved if what we know as civilization is to survive—industrial or class strife, and nationalistic warfare—have challenged the Papacy with new and threatening battle cries. The encyclicals that have issued from the Vatican, beginning with Leo XIII's *Rerum Novarum* in 1891 up to Pius XI's *Divini Redemptoris* in 1937, give evidence of how keenly aware the Papacy is of the attack upon organized religion itself and the necessity for social justice and peace in a world that staggers under the weight of unemployment, debts and armaments. World peace has been the particular goal of Pius XI and he will go down in history, not only as the Pontiff of Reconciliation, but also as the Pope of Peace.

Time and again he has addressed himself to the public by radio, through his encyclicals, by personal appeals. Never more tellingly did his plea ring out than when he spoke to several thousands of war veterans after a Papal mass in San Paolo fuori le Mura. He spoke in French for forty minutes, saying "We pray constantly for peace because the whole world sighs for peace, desires peace, implores peace. We pray for peace because we are the Vicar of Christ who is the King of Peace, who was heralded by the prophets as the Prince of Peace, who when He had come to earth was announced by the angelic canticle of peace to men of good will. As the Vicar of the Divine Master, as the common father of all souls, we pray for peace. *This is our particular and essential duty, without which it is impossible to conceive of a pope.*

"And we desire also, together with peace, that the hopes, exigencies and needs . . . of the people may be recognized and fulfilled and satisfied; with justice and in peace; with justice, because without justice there is only sin and sin renders a people miserable. With justice and in peace, because peace is the absence of all the evils that war brings in its train . . . because peace is the essential condition of all prosperity, the foundation of all that is good in this world, the basis of order and tranquillity.

"May this be the Lord's wish! May God give the world peace—peace made of honor and dignity, of justice and respectable rights, a peace that shall spread happiness and well-being throughout the world."

With the invention of radio the Vatican has been brought nearer to the outside world. Pius XI has made use of this instrument and has spoken his mind in no uncertain terms. If, to the uninitiated, the phraseology of his messages has sounded strange and unfamiliar, there is no question as to his meaning and of the utter sincerity of his dedication.

That Pius chose for his personal motto upon his elevation to the Throne of Peter "*Pax Christi in Regno Christi*" was evidence before the world of the guiding principle of his pontificate, and there can be no doubt that for this cause he would gladly offer up his sufferings in expiation for a distraught world.

LILLIAN BROWNE-OLF.

CONTENTS

BOOK I—DEVELOPMENT

xiii

BOOK II—FULFILMENT

BOOK I
DEVELOPMENT

Chapter I

ACHILLE RATTI'S ORIGIN

IT WAS in the eleventh year of the pontificate of Pius IX (the longest pontificate in Papal history—thirty-two years—) that an Italian bambino first saw the sunlight in the sleepy little town of Desio in Lombardy. Eighteen hundred fifty-seven was to prove a fateful year in Italian history.

Austrian tyranny, after the revolutionary débâcle of 1848, clutched Italy in its relentless grip. The hated Radetsky, Governor-General of the Kingdom of Lombardy-Venetia, was ruling with an iron hand. The Restoration of 1849, following upon the heroic struggles of Garibaldi and Manin, had brought in its wake all the old abuses. An iniquitous tax of one hundred twenty million lire (approximately twenty-five million dollars) a year was levied upon the unfortunate inhabitants of the province. The child's father, Francesco Ratti, must have borne his share of this intolerable burden. He knew, also, how the near-by town of Brescia had been taxed to pay for the very cannon that had bombarded its homes. Only three years before Achille's birth martial law had been proclaimed, the press gagged and women were flogged before the Castello of Milan.

3

The futile efforts of the revolutionaries had cooled the hot temper of the Italian patriots. The calmer counsels of the level-headed Cavour were supplanting the republican dreams of the irreconcilable Mazzini. The new watchword became "Italy and Victor Emmanuel." Garibaldi gave his allegiance to the National Party, composed of various groups of patriots, the year Achille Ratti was born. Daniele Manin signed the Society's *Manifesto* the same year and died after his famous dedication of faith to Piedmont: "Convinced that before everything *Italy must be free*, the republican party says to the House of Savoy, 'Make Italy and I am with you—If not, not.' " This declaration brought thousands of converts to the new standard and gave the reins of leadership to Cavour whose passion to *Make Italy* or *die* was no less fierce than was that of the now abandoned Mazzini.

It was into the midst of these exciting history-making events that the child, Achille Ratti, was born. In the peaceful serenity of the little hamlet, surrounded by the affectionate devotion of simple Italian parents (who was it who said that if children could have their pre-natal desire they would choose Italian parents?) with the far-off Alps gleaming white against the blue sky, the little boy must have often heard the stirring tale of the long struggle to throw off the alien yoke of Austria. But the parents were godly folk and loyal to their Papa Pio. And Pius IX had left the path on which he so bravely started—the path of liberalism and reform—for the conservative path of Papal security.

The high hopes of the Italians in their handsome benevolent Pope seemed justified, when barely a month after his accession he granted an amnesty to the political prisoners languishing in Gregory's dungeons. The enthusiasm of Rome was boundless. The cry "Viva Pio Nono and death to the Austrians!" was heard in every piazza. A fresh wave of religious feeling swept over the countrysides. His alarmed cry "They want to make a Napoleon out of me who am only a poor priest!" reflected his embarrassment at becoming the object of hero worship. Even as late as January, 1847, he granted a decree removing the censorship of the press which resulted in the publication of the *Contemporaneo*, the weekly journal of the democratic party of Rome and the *Felsineo* of Bologna. But, as so often happens, it was the extremists who so terrified the Pope—who had created a consultative Council of State and a Ministry of a more liberal type—as to halt him on the course he was pursuing and finally to turn him back. A burly giant of a man, Angelo Brunetti, with a flair for oratory, pressed upon the Pope when he was driving along the Corso with the cry *Santo Padre, fidatevi nel Popolo*, demanding a civic guard for protection against the centurian outrages. Although Pius granted the guard, it was that arch *bête-noire* of Italy and Europe, Metternich, who, fearing a reforming Papacy, determined to teach Pius a lesson. Troops were dispatched to the Papal city of Ferrara. Though Pius resented the invasion as Pope and as an Italian, though he continued timidly to negotiate for a Customs Union with Tuscany and Piedmont, which seemed to forecast a Federation of Italian States under Pope and King, and to restore the "primacy of Europe" to Italy, though the Council of State did meet in Rome in November comprising among its members the names of famous Risorgimento leaders, yet Pius' speech in addressing the assembly was the first step backward from the popular path.

The well-meaning Pope stood torn between conflicting counsels; for Charles Albert, under popular pressure, had granted a "Statuto" to Piedmont, Ferdinand of Naples had sworn to a constitution, and Leopold of Tuscany had followed suit. It remained only for the Pope to grant the same privilege to the Papal states. He was powerless to ignore the popular demand, and unwilling to compromise his sacred office by granting full powers to a Parliament. When news came that Louis Philippe had fallen, it became certain that Pius IX could delay no longer. The constitutional decree appeared in 1848 and at once it was clear that the claims of the people to self-government and the claims of the Successor of Peter could not be reconciled.

News came to Italy that Vienna had finally risen with the fall of the hated Metternich. This was followed by a council of war in Piedmont. Result: Radetsky's army was defeated in Milan by an unarmed mob. Italy rose to arms and seemed on the point of fulfilling her dreams of freedom as Manin turned out the Austrian garrison in Venice with the loss of a single life!

But the foreign powers, including England, delayed the outcome by endless negotiations with Charles Albert and all was lost by the delay. Radetsky used the precious interval to recoup his forces. Then appeared the Pope's famous Allocution in which he declared that war with Austria was abhorrent to him and that he embraced all princes and peoples in an equal paternal love. Radetsky defeated the Piedmontese and Charles Albert retreated to Milan.

It would be interesting to know how the simple religious people of Lombardy received the news of the Austrian return. Despair and perplexity must have filled the hearts of those loyal folk whose allegiance to the Papacy was a habit and a duty, but who saw their country once more a prey to their alien enemies.

It was in 1857, also, the year of Achille Ratti's birth, that Pius made a tour through his Papal domains; and in Bologna, in bitterness of spirit, bewailed to his former minister against Piedmont "where religion is persecuted and the Church is spared no outrage."

The following year more disrepute was created by Piedmont. Napoleon III called the state "the harborer of assassins" after the attempt on his life by an exile from the Papal states. Felice Orsini, a follower of Mazzini, had thrown a bomb at the Emperor's carriage. Despite this outrage, only three months after Orsini's execution, Napoleon conferred with Cavour and promised him one hundred thousand soldiers, who marched into Piedmont and once again swept the Lombardy plain clean of the hated Austrians.

In spite of the opposition of England, under a conservative ministry, to a war with Austria, Cavour appealed over her head to the Italian youth who answered his secret summons and rushed into Piedmont to join the King's forces, while Garibaldi organized a corps of three thousand volunteers. England demanded the simultaneous disarmament of all three powers, and Napoleon III advised acquiescence; but the canny Cavour held Napoleon to his plighted word. So France declared war on Austria which was just what Cavour had anticipated and worked to achieve. In six weeks Napoleon III and Victor Emmanuel rode in triumph through the streets of Milan. The great city of Lombardy was at last free!

What a thrill must have stirred the towns of the plains, rid, after so many vicissitudes, of the despised Austrian oppressor! Surely the Ratti family in the little neighboring town must have shared in the general rejoicing as if a fresh gust of wind from the Alps had cleansed the air of the miasma of oppression. The father must have gone to his labors with a lighter heart; and his good wife, Teresa, must have rejoiced for her infant son whose future for a freer, happier youth loomed promising and radiant.

But Louis Napoleon became alarmed at the national uprising. He had wanted an Italy of federated states but not a united Italy. Secretly he met with Franz Josef and signed away the fruits of his victory. Victor Emmanuel bowed to necessity, but Cavour resigned the ministry in disgust and went into retirement for six months.

Meanwhile in England the Whigs had come into power; and under the leadership of Lord John Russell and Gladstone demanded that Italy be allowed to work out her own destiny. This declaration of England changed the European picture, and Napoleon III in 1860 abandoned the Federal solution, but at a price. "Re Galantuomo" made the sacrifice of Savoy and of Nice, the birthplace of Garibaldi, with a heavy heart, but the renewed alliance with France kept Austria at bay.

And now Ferdinand II, tyrant of the two Sicilies, the "King Bomba," the "Re Lazzarone," as the Neapolitans contemptuously called him, died at last and another fresh gust of freedom blew from the Mediterranean across the toe and football of Italy. The indefatigable Garibaldi with his famous "thousand" flung themselves against the soldiers of Ferdinand's stupid son, Francis. Under the protection of two British gun-boats they landed at Marsala, defeating a vastly superior force of Neapolitans, marched on to Palermo and in less than two weeks their courage and bluff forced the Neapolitan commander to beg an armistice—just as Garibaldi's last cartridge was fired. Twenty thousand Neapolitan soldiers left Sicily never to return. Francis hastily proclaimed a constitution and begged an alliance with Piedmont. But too late! The subjects of his father had reason to know what a scrap of paper a constitution could be!

King Victor Emmanuel resorted to a ruse which clinched Garibaldi's victory. Out of deference to Napoleon he sent an autographed letter by messenger commanding the General halt at the Straits of Messina, but the messenger carried another secret missive, also autographed by the King, bidding Garibaldi this once to disregard his sovereign's commands. Francis fled to Gaeta while Garibaldi and his Red Shirts marched straight on to Naples, entering the city amidst the wildest demonstrations of enthusiasm. (A plebiscite was held the next year and the Neapolitans voted one million three hundred thousand to ten thousand for "Italy, one and indivisible, with Victor Emmanuel as constitutional King." Sicily's vote was even more overwhelmingly in favor of this objective).

Meanwhile the King's Bersaglieri marched through Umbria and the Marches, successfully defeating the Crusaders (an army recruited in the Papal states and made up of soldiers of every Catholic state in Europe).

The King and Garibaldi met at the little town of Teano. Russia, Prussia, France and Austria damned the work of these two men who had consummated Italy's freedom, but Lord John Russell heartened the Italian patriots with the message "Her Majesty's government see no sufficient reason for the severe censure of Austria, France, Prussia and Russia of the acts of the Sardinian King. Her Majesty's government will turn their eyes rather to the gratifying prospect of a people building up the edifice of their liberties and consolidating the work of their independence."

    ·   ·   ·   ·   ·   ·

In 1864 Pope Pius IX gave out his *Syllabus of Errors*, denying the new and widely heralded idea that a secular state has supreme power and authority over all matters within its boundaries and that each state has a moral obligation to proclaim religious liberty. He condemned free thinkers and agnostics who would destroy the Church; indifferent Christians who would take away the Church's official privileges and limit her status to a private association; the advocates of religious neutrality who would establish lay marriage and lay schools; those who would nationalize the clergy; opponents of the temporal power of the Papacy, and so forth.

In 1869-70 the Pope called the Vatican Council, the first to be held since Trent, three centuries earlier. The doctrine of Papal Infallibility was subscribed to by the vast majority of the eight hundred prelates present, who undoubtedly did not believe they were creating a new doctrine, but felt that they were merely interpreting what had all along been upheld by the Church and had been practiced for centuries. It was not the doctrine, per se, that created opposition by a minority of the bishops, but rather its effect upon the world and its timeliness. For though Protestants denounced it as an affront and a blasphemous assumption, and historians wrote many learned works to show how very fallible some popes had been, the doctrine never meant that a pope cannot sin; but that, in his official pronouncements, when he speaks ex cathedra in the discharge of his episcopal decisions regarding matters of faith and morals, he is given divine assistance by Christ's promise to Peter and is then possessed of that infallibility which the Redeemer gave His Church.

Closely following the hasty adjournment of the Vatican Council, Rome was seized by the victorious troops of the Italian army who made a breach through the wall at Porta Pia, and with the white flag of Papal surrender the temporal power of the Pope was destroyed for sixty years. Henceforth the streets of Rome saw their stately Pontiff no more. Pius IX became a voluntary prisoner of the Vatican.

When this historic event occurred, the boy, Achille Ratti, was thirteen years old, and was already attracting the favorable attention of the good parish priest who taught him and who saw in his young charge a lad of unusual promise and goodly timber for the Church.

.   .   .   .   .   .

Born within sight of the Italian Alps, Achille Ratti's earliest boyhood memories were inevitably tinged and his activities directed by their distant snow-crowned peaks. They beckoned to his imagination with an irresistible appeal. Later, they challenged his hardy spirit to essay those perilous heights whose pinnacles seemed to the reflective lad like Nature's cathedral spires, lifting their arms aloft and pointing their giant fingers to their Maker.

Unacquainted with the sports of a later day with their organized games emphasizing health en masse and developing the competitive instincts, Achille, like other Italian boys of his time, found pleasure in his own self-directed recreation. With a chosen companion or two, or quite alone, the youthful Lombard, with characteristic determination and prudence, hardened his growing limbs on the foothills near Desio; or during the delightful summer months at Uncle Damiano's modest home in the neighboring village of Asso, he roamed at will over the countryside or dreamed of future climbs from the vantage point of the picturesque little village on the jutting brow of Bellagio where Lago di Como reflects the hills in her heavenly mirror, blue as the Virgin's mantle.

His face tanned, his chest expanded, and his legs firm and flexible, the growing youth tasted the delectable fruits of victory on each excursion where a new view opened before his eager eyes. Undoubtedly his whole future life was deeply influenced by this enviable experience of his boyhood days. His mind became self-reliant and observant and his naturally quiet nature found a deep inner satisfaction in each new discovery.

So the environment of Achille Ratti proved suitable and richly satisfying for the normal healthful development of his unique personality. Doubtless a Roman lad of his own day would have surpassed him in quick flashes of repartee, and a Neapolitan gamin in temperamental abandon; but in steady solid achievement, the Lombardy lad seems in retrospect destined by Providence for the mighty tasks that as yet lay hidden in the womb of time.

Thoughtless writers have called Achille Ratti's early environment "drab," and so it might have been to an unimaginative youth; but however placid the boy's nature might appear outwardly, his eyes under the broad brow could kindle with a quick inner response that has never left them.

The ancestral home of the Ratti was Rogeno, a little

sprawling town on the foothills of the upper Brianza,
midway between Como and Lecco, overlooking Pian
d'Erba and Lake Pusiano. It is one of those numerous
picturesque villages covered with coral and tawny-
colored villas, and crowned with umbrella pines and
cypresses. At its foot is spread a carpet of green meadows
all the way to the foothills of the Alps. In direct line
the first Ratti mentioned in the register is Gerolamo,
whose first child was born in 1616. For many years the
family members are designated as *contadini;* later, with
the development of the silk industry in the region, they
are registered as textile workers.

They were a hardy, long-lived folk. Manzoni, a famous
son of the region, has written a novel [1] in which he has
immortalized the people he knew. He pictures them as
pious, hard-working and simple; a type characteristic of
the Lombardy farmers into which the Ratti were born.
As the family prospered, some of its members felt a civic
pride in their town and enlarged the parish church. The
cemetery was beautified. One of the finest day-nurseries
for miles around was founded by a Ratti.

Francesco Ratti, Achille's father, had several temporary residences, due to the fluctuations in the silk
trade in which he was actively interested as manager
and later as part-owner. He had married Teresa Galli
of Soronno and was made manager of the Conti
Brothers silk-mill at Pusiano. Here he continued for
ten years. We next find him at Carugate in the Riva

[1] Manzoni, Alessandro (1785-1873), *I promessi sposi: storia Milanese
del secolo XVII* (Fratelli Rechiedei, Milano).

factory, then at Pinerolo in Piedmont. At the time of his death in 1881 he was living with his growing family at Pertusella, employed in the Gadda silk-mill of which he was part-owner.

Ambrogio Damiano Achille, the fourth child of Francesco and Teresa, was born at Desio, another of the silk industry towns in the district of Monza, on the edge of the Brianza which is a health resort, high and beautiful, for well-to-do Milanese. Desio boasts three buildings that dominate the scene and life of the little town—the large parish church with its fine cupola which stands on the piazza into which all the crooked streets converge, the splendid Villa Traversi, later bought by the Tittoni, and the large silk factory of the Gavazzi Brothers, an important center of the silk business of Lombardy.

Achille, as he came to be called, was ushered into life on the last day of May, eighty-one years ago. The next day he was baptized in the parish church. Although Desio's pride in her now famous son is well justified, we have seen how the happy coincidence was due solely to the accidents of his father's trade.

Desio is in the diocese of Milan and from the great city it receives its religious complexion; but it is also a self-sustaining little community, supplying its own wants within its own confines. Formerly a sheep-raising community, it had gradually turned to the successful growing of mulberries for the cultivation of silk-worms. Before Achille was born the pastoral village was being transformed into an industrial center, small but prosperous. The necessity of finding a market for their trade created a wider outlook among the inhabitants of what had been a sleepy little hamlet, bringing into the busy little town a new spirit of enterprise and expansion. Achille's father was manager of the local factory, and while he never became affluent, the family did not know want and his position in the town was assured and respected. The father of five children was able to give all of his sons a good education, keeping three of them in schools of higher learning at the same time.

Achille was only ten years of age when he completed his studies under the guidance of the estimable parish priest, Don Giuseppe Volontieri, who for forty-three years gave elementary instruction in his own house to all the parish boys. The good priest had watched young Ratti with especial interest, for he was an exceptional teacher who knew by instinct which of his charges would bear fruit from the seed he had planted. And although Achille was the merest child when he left Don Giuseppe's, he remembered the kind old man gratefully, and when the old priest died in 1884, his former pupil, Professor Ratti now, delivered the funeral oration in the public piazza of Desio before all the people and wrote the lines on his tombstone in the cemetery.

Leaving his former playmates, the boy was entered at San Pietro Martire to complete a secondary, or as we would say, a high school, course. All the teachers at San Pietro's were clerics and his studies were the equivalent of what an endowed English school of the time offered; English, French, Latin and the sciences—that is, mathematics and geology, etc. Mathematics he has always considered a relaxing pastime. While religious instruction was strictly ecclesiastical, it was only one branch of learning. As yet Achille had not definitely decided upon his future career, although his former teacher, Don Volontieri, the parish priest of Desio, and Don Damiano Ratti, his uncle of Asso, both had their secret hopes. But they prudently refrained from urging the Church's claims, or from influencing his decision. In fact, Uncle Damiano later showed his nephew all the sacrifices and difficulties such a life entails when Achille finally made known his choice of a career to that worthy priest.

The youngsters of Italy mature much younger than English or American boys who seem to have a more prolonged childhood, and are, in comparison, far behind Italian youths of their own age in their accomplishments and achievements. Always self-contained and reserved, here at San Martire's Achille became more studious and apart. His companions were few but congenial. All his life they have meant much more to him, and in after years have retained a stronger hold upon his affections, than is perhaps the case when they are more indiscriminately chosen.

Achille had hardly reached puberty when he came across a copy of Milton's *Paradise Lost* in Italian. The work teased and fascinated him and he spent countless hours over the thumb-worn pages—this at an age when the book in the original scarcely attracts Anglo-Saxon youths. It was while he was puzzling over the volume that he had his first opportunity to take a trip into the heart of the Alps and satisfy a growing longing to really explore the majestic peaks.

En route his party came across another party, one of whose members was an English clergyman. The two groups got into conversation and for the first time in his life the boy, Achille, heard the language of Milton spoken by an Englishman. His active mind was tantalized as he listened wonderingly. On his return to Desio he had made a fixed resolve. He would master the English tongue. His mother, Teresa, watched her son bent over strange books with scowling brow, spending hours wrestling with curious-looking words and oblivious of physical discomfort, quite forgetting to eat. But, like Mary of old, she did not interfere, but pondered these things in her heart.

Indeed, the household seemed run without coercion or tyranny. For, although the father, Francesco, had with his compatriot Lombardians determined to ensure the perpetuity of their guilds by training their sons in their crafts—there was always the exception of the priestly career. Signor Ratti was in his day singularly free from despotic control over his children. The parents seemed to rule with gentle firmness and Christian patience, unencumbered by any modern theories of the psychology of child training.

At last the youth's hours of laborious effort were rewarded by his being able to read some of the simpler passages of Milton in the original.

This first excursion into the Alps also quickened his desire for further climbs. The urge to behold the marvels of nature from great heights, and the challenge to his growing manhood to overcome obstacles and tame the frowning pinnacles by sheer will and fortitude were at work within his adventurous spirit.

Later he tried to put into words the impressions he had experienced and the beauty he had beheld. But as yet the secrets of nature were too terrible. He was awe-struck and silent before the miracles of God.

But it was during the summer months with Uncle Damiano Ratti, the parish priest and provost of Asso, that he drank in that deep quietude of spirit that seems to have been his ultimate need. It was this good uncle who made his plastic mind responsive to the dignity of the beauty and order of the Church. This was no slavish submission on the boy's part, but a perfectly natural acceptance of the law of obedience to the orthodox Faith. Here at Asso, gazing dreamily across the shimmering blue of Como, watching the sails of the orange fishing craft bellying in the breeze as they sought a more favored haven among the coves of the lake, his eyes travelled across the blue expanse. He saw the mountains looming in the distance beyond the opposite shore and felt their mystical spell.

For many consecutive summers he returned to Asso, finding in his uncle's house a second home. Here his formative years were molded and his receptive spirit fed on the unparalleled beauty of his surroundings. This continuity of spiritual sustenance stamped the developing youth with deep quiet powers that in after years in the midst of a noisy world have set him apart as a tower of strength.

Achille was thirteen and still at San Martire's when Rome was taken by the national troops and Pius IX went into self-imposed solitude in the Vatican. Yet he was old enough to realize what the imprisonment of the Supreme Pontiff meant to the religion he loved and practiced, and to the dignity and prestige of the Papacy. Lombardy and Piedmont were undergoing a small industrial revolution, a backwash of what England and Europe generally had been experiencing. The spiritual conflicts which always accompany vast economic and social changes were felt by the young students. The reflection of these changes in the religious realm created a spirit of intransigence; controversies bitter and heated strove for supremacy. Pius IX had been compelled to take a decisive stand against the tide of "modernism" and yet a progressive Catholicism could not be ignored. A spirit was in the air that no Papal pronouncement could retard.

For a hundred years the Papal power had been encroached upon. Now at last in 1870 it became a mere shadow of its former glory and prestige. The youth, Achille, had been grounded in strict Catholic doctrine by the pious priest of Asso. He had imbibed an unquestioning faith in the Spiritual Ruler in Rome. He believed with all his soul that the Supreme Pontiff must be independent of all earthly authority. But he was a patriotic Italian, loving his country as only an Italian can. The vital concern, the Roman Question, became overnight an absorbing interest to his young mind. He began the study of the history of the Papacy with a new keen zest. Contemporary church history became more than an academic interest—this at a time when the average American boy knows and cares less for anything more vital than baseball, and is quite incapable of applying his mind to the consideration of large impersonal concerns.

Was Ratti aware of the dangers to the Faith in the new spirit of intransigence? Did the motto *Faith without Fear* which he took when he was ordained, indicate a realization of the perilous path he himself must tread within the ranks of the clergy? Often he had listened to the excited young students debate the Roman Question. It was remembered afterward that he never participated in these debates, but merely listened with a far-off expression in his deep-set intent eyes. Doubtless he had not made up his mind on the ever-recurrent question; or if he had, it was formulating slowly, and he was not yet ready to commit himself until he was quite sure of his position.

Chapter II

THE PRIESTLY STUDENT

DURING the summer holidays at Don Damiano Ratti's home at Asso, the young nephew of that superior man met many priests and youthful students. One can imagine the stimulating discussions that took place concerning the condition of the Church and the troubled times through which Italy was passing. The worthy priest's house assumed something of the character of a seminary; for Achille's uncle, Don Damiano, attracted to himself the intellectually élite, since he was the type of man who would have filled any position he held with distinction. Even in the comparatively restricted post he occupied at Asso, he built a hospital and day-nursery; and later gave of himself without stint to the cholera sufferers in 1886, for which service he received the Cross of the Order of the Crown of Italy. Among those who enjoyed the hospitality of this truly remarkable man was the Archbishop of Milan, Monsignor Calabiana, whose observant eyes had watched the youthful student. He was much impressed by Achille's quiet composure and maturity.

After completing the course of study at the Ginnasio di San Martire, young Ratti, due to Mgr. Calabiana's guidance, was entered at the Seminary of Monza in the same diocese, where he remained for two years. Here he confirmed the judgment of his uncle and the Archbishop so gratifyingly that he went on to the Collegio di San Carlo Borromeo in Milan.

The saintly influence of St. Charles Borromeo permeates the Milanese seminaries and his wise rule still regulates the institutions of the archdiocese. These schools are noted for the methods used to prepare young students for the priesthood. Those who know say they combine secular studies and religious subjects; these, together with the spiritual discipline they impose, result in forming exceptional pastors of souls. "They do not suppress," says the Reverend Angelo Novelli, "but develop and direct the characteristic traits of their students." [1] A genuine fraternity among the pupils from all classes of society creates a spirit of real democracy.

Many of Don Ratti's fellow students at San Carlo's were of the aristocracy and consequently better acquainted with the ways of the world than he. Their culture impressed the son of the bourgeois silk merchant. Without imitating their polished suavity he learned ease of manner. His sensitive adaptability took from them what he needed and made it his own. A rare, almost intuitive sympathy that can put the self-conscious at their ease, due to native kindness and goodness of heart, combined with a cultivated urbanity, have created a personality that knows how to soothe and charm.

Mgr. Luigi Talamoni, later professor of history at the

[1] Pio XI. Casa Editrice "Pro Familia." Milano.

Monza seminary, was young Ratti's teacher of philosophy at San Carlo's. "He was an exceptional student," says the Monsignor, "both in his learning and in his influence on all of his companions. I was obliged to come well prepared to classes where I had such a wonderful pupil."

Ratti and his friend, Alessandro Lualdi, (later Archbishop of Palermo) were conspicuous for their application at the Collegio. Though they did not take vows, they assisted the Archbishop in religious duties and in clerical work.

Young Ratti's memory was so remarkable that he did not rely upon notes during lectures and could easily discourse on theology, philosophy and canon law from the material he had stored away in his mind. In mathematics, too, he outshone all the others—so much so that for a time his superiors thought seriously of sending him to Turin to specialize in that department of science. But Providence and his own inclination led elsewhere!

During all his years of preparation Don Ratti had been blessed with perfect health. He was, and has remained, an outdoor man. His robust constitution made it easy for him to devote himself to his studies with closer and more sustained application than was possible, or perhaps advisable, for the average youth of his age. His companions used to come to him at San Carlo's and protest against his prolonged absorption in his books. But he would only smile and declare that he did not know fatigue, and that if he needed relaxation he had only to turn to a mathematical problem, having discovered for himself that a change of mental activity was as soothing and beneficial as loafing and chatting.

This independence was characteristic of all his actions. His was not a gregarious nature. Yet his capacity for friendship was deep and genuine. The few choice spirits that gravitated to him have held a warm place in his memory. His nature, even as a youth, was not what is called "expansive." His personality from his boyhood days has remained deep and quiet like a pool of still water—more like a steady stream that flows slowly on its destined course; widening and deepening as it nears the ocean. The years have brought confidence and power. So he was singularly free during adolescence from what is now called "mass-psychology." There seemed to be an inner spring back of all his actions and decisions. He managed to keep his individuality intact and to preserve the integrity of his personality; this in spite of a community life that too often breeds uniformity—a sort of common denominator of conduct and mentality.

But we have said that San Carlo's was no ordinary college. When his school companions would chide him on his aloofness, his winning smile would dispel resentment and his unaffected sigh, "There is so much to learn and some appear to learn it quicker than others!" would completely disarm them. Such a comment, they knew, was only in self-defense. Never did he consciously try to dictate to others. There was no sting in his words.

So we can picture the young student's days filled to the brim with lectures, serious studies, and regular hours of hard-earned rest in the cell-like room of the dormitory. Or we can see his erect and elastic figure—well-built, but not tall—starting off for the countryside, alone, or with Lualdi by his side, walking with the easy stride of an accomplished climber, his head held high as he inhaled deep breaths of the sweet Lombardy air.

Already the qualities of independence and stability that have characterized Pius XI were apparent to his friends and the good Archbishop. There were reserves of power in the quiet-faced youth. At the termination of his career at San Carlo's, Don Achille Ratti's progress was summed up by one of his professors as wholly satisfactory—and, indeed, as "brilliant." The Archbishop needed no further proof of the young man's fitness for the priesthood. His friend, Lualdi, had distinguished himself in theology. A dream that must have been shared between them was to be realized. They were ready for Rome.

The Collegio Lombardo at Rome had just been reopened by Leo XIII after being closed for eight years, following the upheaval of 1870, and was under the supervision of the Bishop of Crema, Monsignor Ernesto Fontana. This was their logical destination.

In Rome the youthful student must have responded eagerly to the tremendous appeal of the Eternal City. There unfolded to his keen mind a fuller realization of the meaning of the history of the Church. Here in the catacombs was the very cradle of Christianity. All the magnificent basilicas and ancient sites spoke eloquently of the continuous story that harked back to the

Apostles, Peter and Paul. This cumulative wealth of Christian experience could not fail to exercise a potent influence on an ardent young believer of the One True Faith. For if this dynamo of spiritual power fires the imagination of even the unbelieving sojourner in Rome, we can conceive of what its message must be to one who participates intimately in its regenerative graces. For it is as true today as it was during the pontificate of Gregory XVI when in 1840 Macaulay wrote the words: "The Papacy remains, not in decay, not a mere antique; but full of life and youthful vigor."

To one endowed with the historic sense, the spectacle of a throng of fifty thousand souls from every corner of the globe, speaking every language on earth, standing at reverent attention, eager eyes turned toward the great right door leading to the throne room of St. Peter's, expectantly waiting for the supreme moment when the trumpets shall announce the Vicar of Christ Himself, borne aloft on the *sedia gestatoria* for all the world to behold and partake of the pontifical blessing which the vast throng with a single impulse kneels to receive—there is no experience on earth like it in solemnity and spiritual elevation. It is the symbol of the Church Triumphant!

How many times young Ratti must have participated in silent awe in the impressive ceremony, as Leo XIII, a Pontiff venerable in years and wisdom, slight and frail of build, raised his long thin fingers in the familiar gesture of the sign of the cross. Only in recent years has the true greatness of this truly distinguished Pope begun to be appreciated by the world generally. Did the youthful student for the priesthood, arriving in Rome at a time of great moment for the Church, realize amidst what tremendous events he was moving? It is more than likely that he did, for his analytical mind was enriched by much study. From the beginning he was an eager student of contemporary history. He must have responded to the tempo of the times.

For Pius IX's long pontificate had seen a bitter struggle between the Holy See and the alarming revolutionary forces of Europe. The rampant anti-clerical phobia presaged an anxious future for the Church. An era had passed; and the alert, far-seeing mind of Leo was grappling with the new problems that seemed to be dominated by purely sectarian interests. One cannot doubt how indelibly imprinted upon young Ratti's memory must have been the shameful insult to the body of Pius IX when, as it was borne to its final resting place in San Lorenzo fuori le Mura, ruffians attempted to seize it and throw it into the Tiber.

Yet, however outraged his soul may have been over this indignity to the person of the Pope, Ratti was not to be numbered among the irreconcilables. He was too well-informed and too canny not to know that the old days, once gone, never return. A new *modus vivendi* for the Church and the State of Italy must be found. Hating anarchy and desiring above all else a stable social peace, his nature naturally sought a more Christian solution of the impossible dilemma. He must have recognized that the arm of the Lord is far-reaching and that the regime of Leo was decreed by God to regain a new dignity and prestige for the Church. For there can be no doubt, in retrospect, and writing after the event, that the Papacy under Leo XIII had entered upon a renaissance which has continued and is today at flood-tide.

Young Ratti and his friend, Lualdi, were both in their twenty-third year when they entered the Lombard College in Rome. Three months later Ratti was ordained priest in St. John Lateran, his father and brother, Fermo, being present and receiving his first blessing. The following day he celebrated Mass in the church of the Lombards, San Carlo al Corso, where the heart of the saint is enshrined. Two years later, in 1882, after attending courses in canon law, he took his degree, at the Gregorian University. In the same year he completed his work and took his degree in theology at the Sapienza, and in philosophy at the Academia di San Tommaso.

Monsignor Fontana had introduced Ratti and Lualdi to His Holiness on one of the Pontiff's visits to this child of his spirit (San Tommaso's). Later Leo undoubtedly kept the youths in mind as they were the first students to matriculate at the Academy where he had established the courses in the Thomist philosophy in which he took such keen personal interest. It was a red-letter day indeed when the two young doctors were summoned into the Holy Father's presence to receive the Pontiff's congratulations upon their successful achievements. For the Pope's solicitude for these two chosen vessels into which the rare old wisdom had been poured was so great that he sent by special messenger an invitation to his protégés to come to the Vatican for a private audience.

Undoubtedly this personal contact with a living Pope exerted a lasting influence upon the young theologian just as the revival of the Thomist philosophy must have wrought a decisive impression upon his mind. This was a vital contribution of a living Pope to a future Pope that neither could have foreseen at the time.

We can imagine with what awe the two youths prepared themselves for the momentous occasion. Leo had come in from his gardens and was about to enter the Clementine Hall in his sedan chair when he saw the two young men. When told who they were, he asked to be left unattended, and he blessed the young doctors who had fallen on their knees before his chair. If one endowed with prophetic vision could have observed this historic incident, how impressive the scene would have appeared as the great Pontiff of the new regime, Leo XIII, extended his arm in blessing over the future Pope who was to break the fetters of Papal imprisonment for himself and all popes thereafter, and restore to the Papacy, after sixty years of struggle, the old temporal power.

The venerable and saintly Pontiff did not leave the young men after the Papal blessing, but discoursed with them at length upon their achievements and on the true philosophy of religion, and their obligation to Saint Thomas Aquinas to extend the influence of their Christian scholarship throughout the world. How potent were the Holy Father's words uttered at such a moment and under such circumstances to two such eager young souls, full of ardor for the cause of the Church to which they were dedicating their lives!

For over three years young Ratti had been in Rome, imbibing not only the philosophy of St. Thomas, but a wealth of knowledge about the Church and applied religion as it affected the lives of the average citizen of the Eternal City, a knowledge of the strained relationship between the Vatican and the Quirinal and of a thousand and one other practical matters of daily concern to an ardent churchman and patriotic Italian.

At last his old friend and advisor from Milan, the Archbishop, Cardinal Calabiana, sent for his protégé to return home and accept the curacy of the little village of Barni, on the shores of Lake Como. Thus Providence brought Father Ratti back to the scenes of his origin; but what a different man he returned from the provincial youth who, a decade earlier, had left those placid shores!

What an opportunity to assimilate the wealth of knowledge and experience of which he had so eagerly partaken in the Eternal City! In the quiet of the long evenings his thoughts returned to Rome with clarified vision, and there came to him a fuller sense of the tremendous meaning of all that he had learned and observed there. Amid the peaceful surroundings of the simple folk of his parish he learned to correlate and clarify the vast erudition he had imbibed at San Tommaso's. Most of all, in that detached mood that is so essential to the creation of a just perspective, the Roman Question pressed upon his mind for a solution.

But the contemplation of all that he had seen and heard at Rome was not to end in sterile thoughts. Within the space of only a few months, the good Archbishop, who watched over him so lovingly, called him to Milan. In 1883, in his twenty-sixth year, Father Ratti accepted an appointment as Professor of Sacred Eloquence and Dogmatic Theology at San Carlo's. Here he remained for five years. The young students under his care all testify how stimulating were his lectures, how learned and sound his teaching, and with what charming courtesy he encouraged their studies. They recall his fine artistic taste and speak of his deep religious convictions.

Because of the tact and wisdom he displayed among his students, it is not surprising that his success as a teacher, and more especially his ever-increasing scholarship, should be rewarded with his appointment to fill a vacancy among the doctors of the Ambrosian Library in Milan under its illustrious Prefect, the Abate Ceriani.

.   .   .   .   .   .

When Father Ratti arrived at the Ambrosiana to assist its Prefect, Ceriani, that renowned Orientalist of the famous old library was carrying on with unstinted devotion the tradition of learning of a long line of distinguished savants. For three centuries the library had grown in fame through the acquisition of rare manuscripts, books, and costly works of art, until it was recognized by serious students as one of the few great libraries of the world—in the same class as the Vatican Library of Rome, the Nationale of Paris, and the British Museum of London. The history of learning is preserved and enriched by such selfless scholars as Ceriani, whose names are known only to the elect, yet whose sacrifices and consecration to the cause of true culture make it live on in an indifferent age, in spite of the modern tendency to belittle and degrade it. In Dr. Ratti, Ceriani found a scholar after his own heart, who, for nineteen long years, was to work under him, assisting him in his researches; travelling abroad on missions in search of some old tome, to unearth some ancient manuscript, to confer with other scholars and to address societies for the further glory of their mutual labors.

No library in the world has a nobler history than the Ambrosian. Founded in the Late Renaissance (1609) by Cardinal Federigo Borromeo, a cousin of the great St. Charles Borromeo and his successor in the Milanese See, it was the personal expression of this remarkable man. Manzoni has left a perfect picture of the founder and of all the details of the foundation and the methods by which the numerous duties of its officers were carried on.

Although so frugal in his personal life as to seem miserly the founder of the Ambrosiana "planned with such munificent liberality, to supply which with books and manuscripts, besides the preservation of those he had already collected with great labor and expense, he sent eight of the most learned and experienced men he could find, to make purchases throughout Italy, France, Spain, Germany, Flanders, Greece, Lebanon and Jerusalem. By this means he succeeded in gathering together about thirty thousand printed volumes, and fourteen thousand manuscripts. To this library he united a college of doctors . . . whom he maintained at his charge while he lived. . . . Their office was to cultivate various branches of study; theology, history, literature, and the Oriental languages; each one being obliged to publish some work on the subject assigned to him. He also added a college he called Trilingue, for the study of the Greek, Latin and Italian languages; a college of pupils for instruction in these several languages that they might become professors in their turn; a press for the Oriental languages;—that is, Hebrew, Persian and Armenian; a gallery of paintings, another of statues and a school for the three principal arts of design." [2]

Of the nine professors he supported out of his personal funds, eight were selected from the pupils of the seminary, indicating how sound and well-grounded he considered their instruction and the high standard attained by his college of doctors. For the use and perpetuity of the library he left ample provision at his death, showing how far-sighted his vision and how dear to his heart the Ambrosiana had become. He required that his librarian should keep up an extended correspondence with the most learned men of Europe, to bring to him all the latest information on all the works of science and the best works on any subject that had been published. Such books were immediately purchased for the library. His labors were not only "admirable, but judicious and elegant" and far beyond the ideas and habits of his age.

[2] From *The Betrothed*, Chap. 22, English Translation, New York, 1899.

Most remarkable of all, this exceptional man of his time ordered that the books preserved here should be accessible to all, whether citizens of Lombardy or strangers. Books were brought to anyone who should demand them, with full opportunity to sit down and study them, with the provision of pen, ink, and paper, to take notes. Although today these facilities are approximated in all good libraries, in the seventeenth century such an innovation was unheard of, for in most libraries of Europe all valuable books were concealed under lock and key and the public had no access to them. No one can properly appraise the effect upon scholarship of this method of making all books available to any student who might desire them. The greater part of the Cardinal's fortune was consumed by his devotion to his beloved enterprise. Thus the beginning of a rich legacy of wisdom from all the ages was given to the world.

Many works famous in the history of literature have been created because of the generosity of Cardinal Borromeo. Distinguished men of learning like Giggi, Muratori, Angelo Mai, Sassi, Oltrocchi, and last, but not least, the Abate Ceriani himself, under whom Dr. Ratti worked, have added glory to the famous old institution, so that today the library is a Mecca to which scholars from all over the world are indebted.

Here, in the silence dedicated to learning, Dr. Ratti worked and wrote, conscientiously following in the revered footsteps of its founder and his famous successors. For nineteen years he was the obedient disciple and loving son of the elderly Ceriani whose reputation for discipline and petulance over any inefficiency have come down to us, along with his self-abnegation of spirit and devotion to his cherished library.

The many subjects Dr. Ratti contributed for such Milanese journals as the *Archivio storico lombardo, Rendiconti dell' Instituto lombardo di scienze e lettere, Giornale storico letteratura italiana, Scuola Cattolica,* etc., dealt with history, biology, liturgy, hagiography, politics, art and archeology. But all these related to the Ambrosian church and had to do with Milanese history. It is his native Lombardy, its famous metropolis, and its glorious church that claim his hours of research and writing. Over seventy of these studies are analyzed by Senator Malvezzi in his *Pio XI nei suoi scritti* published in 1923 by Treves Frères.

Dr. Ratti's intellectual interests were vast and varied. Whether he is engaged in writing on art such as his monograph on an ancient mosaic in the basilica of St. Ambrose; or in contributing important data in his biographical study of St. Charles Borromeo [3] or in deciphering some old palimpsest, or in archeological research as in his article on a Latin inscription of the first century, found in Milan in 1904, or in editing his *Missale Ambrosianum Duplex*, he is always original in his approach and impartial in his treatment of the facts. Never does the apologist blind the faithful historian. His philosophical approach to history, which he firmly believed to be "the living tissue of facts wherein the thoughts and deeds of men and God unite, mix and

---

[3] *San Carlo Borromeo e il III centenario della sua canonizzazione.*

cross each other" so that a "marvelous providential plan is wrought" in which "the love of God for man is manifest," pervades all his written work, whether he writes as critic, linguist, paleographer or archeologist.

But it was not only as a writer of distinction that the famous librarian achieved renown. He is remembered today for the help he so generously gave to students, lavishly bestowing upon them the benefits of his vast learning. His fluency with languages was of great assistance in this task of acting as host and guide and counsellor. And it was not only to those who were studying in the library in Milan that his services were rendered. He answered at great length all inquiries that came to him in writing from any land, giving adequate and exact information. The Prefect of the Laurentian Library of Florence, Enrico Rostagno, declares that there are few scholars in Italy or abroad who have not consulted Dr. Ratti and been benefitted by his courteous helpfulness both when he was doctor and Prefect of the Ambrosiana and later as Prefect of the Biblioteca Vaticana at Rome. Many students can testify today in their own behalf of the resources that have been provided and the facilities that have been made available by this self-effacing scholar.

There is yet another gift, as essential as those already mentioned, which the great librarian must possess, which was conspicuous in Dr. Ratti—that of administrator. Important reforms were instituted under his wise direction. He made of the Ambrosiana a living, pulsating organism, planning and overseeing the reorganization of its many departments. As Prefect he provided a special room for the invaluable manuscripts and drawings of Leonardo da Vinci. He opened the Gallery of Arms, and the Rose Gallery with its exhibit of engravings of the history of Milan, and also the Museo Settala. He wrote a guide of the thoroughly modernized institution, with a history of the Library and a full description of its art treasures. This executive faculty was later to be allowed full scope in the field of practical diplomacy. For his scholarly work and administrative achievements as Doctor and Prefect of the Ambrosiana, Dr. Ratti had conferred upon him the Cross of the Order of Sts. Maurice and Lazarus by the Italian government.

Ratti's relationship with Ceriani under whom he worked was most intimate and affectionate. The famous old Orientalist treated him as his own son. Between the two men, so different in temperament and age, but so alike in their enthusiasm in behalf of learning, there existed perfect respect and enduring admiration. Ceriani's temper was known to be uncertain. He was impatient of all that distracted him from his work. His one passion was his library. His unconcern of personal preferment was as genuine as it was rare. Young Ratti soon discovered beneath the cold exterior the humility of a great spirit; his Superior's lack of urbanity was a protective covering that camouflaged a heart of gold. And Ceriani recognized in his assistant a devotion to learning and a willingness for self-abnegation that answered a responsive chord in his lonely old heart. A deep affection grew up between these two men so unlike in temperament and years. The younger became the confessor of the older. His letters to his Superior are more than mere discussions about their mutual labors. There are tender inquiries concerning his health, and beautiful allusions to the deep concern he felt for the elderly man. When the great scholar died, Ratti took charge of his funeral and erected a tablet to his memory in the old library in which they had worked together for two decades. Each year he led a pilgrimage to Ceriani's tomb.

During the years of Dr. Ratti's incumbency at the Milanese Library, time had not stood still. Entering in 1888 in his thirty-first year, he passed through middle age under Ceriani, and beyond that period he was still working there as Prefect for another seven years, until His Holiness, Pius X, called him to Rome to act as Pro-Prefect under Father Ehrle at the Vatican Library. Here, at the Ambrosiana, we see him, immersed in the atmosphere of books, moving silently among the students and visitors from the outside world, or seated in calm seclusion at his desk, ready at a moment's notice to leave his own literary labors to give advice, direct some stranger, act as guide to some party of English or American tourists. To keep himself from growing stale in the cloistered serenity of peaceful walls, he acted as chaplain to the nuns of the Cenacolo (the Cenacle), an order that takes care of poor Milanese children. To this function of pastor of souls (a duty he performed for thirty years!) he added the self-imposed task of instructing the street urchins and chimney-sweeps of the city in the catechism and becoming intimately acquainted with their individual lives and needs. The fastidious scholar, careful of dress, spectacled, grave of manner, lavished upon these dirty little charges the same earnest attention and kindly practical assistance that he bestowed upon the eminent scholars that sought him out.

Training for the priesthood, self-discipline imposed as a religious duty, innate serenity and adjustability, diversions of mountain climbing, visits abroad and contact with some of the best minds in the world, mental adventures in books, the passion of discovery in the field of literature—yes! and the romance of the religious life itself—all these Dr. Ratti knew and experienced at firsthand. For the Monsignor, as he had become, was not one of those priests who grow apathetic in their religion. In him it has always remained the mainspring of his being; directing, consoling, fortifying his hours of doubt and weariness. Daily he finds his Source of Strength in the Holy Eucharist. Like any layman he feels the need of confession. On his mountain adventures he carries his breviary and recites his prayers. But his vision of his God is not limited to the book, nor even to the Mass. He sees Him in the sunrise at dawn, enveloped in glory. He hears His terrible voice in the thundering avalanche. He receives a direct revelation of Him in the pure mystery of the snow and in the peaceful beauty of Lago di Como.

It must not be imagined that the scholarly doctor was deprived by his clerical dress of the amenities of cultivated society. Some of the best Milanese families invited him to their homes. They were proud to have him grace their tables. His quiet ease of manner, his vast scholarship, his latent wit and infinite tact, made him a welcome guest. He could banish self-consciousness with his gracious smile and genial word. He did not appear pedantic, nor overladen with learning. Yet, when the occasion demanded, he could be non-committal and relapse into a smiling silence. If the subject of conversation became controversial this was his habitual demeanor. For he preferred to be an interested listener rather than to override an opponent. Argumentative disputation on such questions as the Roman issue left him silent and attentive. Aggressiveness and self-assertiveness, heated controversy and the mania to outshine others were as alien to his nature as conflict and mob violence were hateful. He was, and has remained, a man of peace.

. . . . . .

In 1894, five years after Father Ratti was called to the Ambrosiana, his old friend, Cardinal-Archbishop Calabiana, who had seen the boy Achille grow to manhood and justify all his expectations, died. He was succeeded by the saintly Ferrari as head of the diocese of Milan— the largest and one of the most difficult in the world to administer. The Cardinal, impressed by the scholarship and character of the Doctor of the Ambrosiana, began to entrust him with responsibilities outside the library walls. He turned to him to carry forward the work of re-establishing religious instruction in the public schools. It was a task requiring the utmost tact as, for several years, priests had been excluded by law from the schools in Milan. Over a hundred priests volunteered their ser-

vices to Dr. Ratti and the scheme created such opposition by the anti-clerical elements that only through the
consummate wisdom of their leader was the plan exe-
cuted and continued.

Because of Dr. Ratti's success in this very delicate
matter, Cardinal Ferrari continued to call upon him;
and his own health failing, leaned upon his lieutenant
more and more. On Ceriani's death Dr. Ratti was made
his successor as Professor of Hebrew and was later appointed canon of the Church of St. Ambrose with the
title of "Monsignor." Today the visitor is shown by the
guide the stone seat the present Pontiff occupied for
several years as canon under the shadow of the fourth
century pulpit from which it is said St. Ambrose
preached and converted St. Augustine.

Cardinal Ferrari and his Monsignor were in complete
accord regarding the necessity of fostering the growth
of *Azione Cattolica*. Monsignor Ratti's admiration for
his Cardinal was unbounded. At the third centenary of
the canonization of St. Charles Borromeo, the quiet
priestly scholar forgot his restraint and spoke with the
warmth and enthusiasm of a devoted disciple.

Because he is of gold unalloyed, boundless in charity, inexhaustible in zeal, untiring in labor, truly great in virtues . . .
we needs must admire, love and imitate him. And he can count
on us, on our work, on our lives—[continues the fervent disciple,
adding with the firm conviction of one who knows]: in the
battle for ideas, for truth, for souls, the work of books has its
place and its value. The soldier of truth, coming back from the
firing-line, his ammunition spent, knows that the man of books

may point out new and untouched shores; [for] . . . there is an eighth sacrament, the Sacrament of Learning, which Saint Francis de Sales called the sacrament par excellence for the priest.

And there are those who have called Achille Ratti phlegmatic!

Milan has long been the arena for conflicting intellectual opinions, and has always resounded with the clamor of party strife. Achille Ratti did not participate in party controversy. Yet on the occasion of the riot in May of 1898 he braved the armed soldiery in the streets of Milan to reach the police station where the Capuchins had been arrested and plead for their release, explaining they had not participated in the Socialist uprising which had resulted in over a hundred deaths, but had merely offered sanctuary to fleeing rioters. Feeling keenly that the true mission of the priest is peace, and that his position in the old and honored institution of learning placed him above party alliances which might injure his usefulness as a public servant, Ratti was a consistent advocate of sanity. This aloofness from party alignment was later to prove a great factor in his election to the Papacy when the qualities he possessed were sadly needed in a war-racked world.

Ratti neither posed as an advocate of "science" nor did he identify himself with those intemperate devotees of the Church's "rights" to the exclusion of sanity and charity. In regard to the Roman Question he was neither with the Intransigents nor with the so-called "Liberals" who sought peace at any price. He was too good an

Italian not to desire above all things a reconciliation in which his love for his Church and his love for his country might be harmoniously merged.

During all the years of Achille Ratti's residence in Milan he kept in close touch with his relatives—especially with his brothers and nephews. His mother, long a widow, lived with her daughter, Camilla, in the Via Nerone, and he visited her almost daily. His feeling of reverence for her is one that is commonly observed and is often wondered at by travelers from countries where the worship of the Virgin Mary is not practiced, but which is soon discovered by foreigners to be characteristic of Italian sons toward their mothers in the flesh. Certain it is that Dr. Ratti almost worshiped his widowed mother. In a dedication to a learned work dealing with Milanese history he writes of her:

To you, mother of a rare and ancient type, I dedicate these plans—the oldest known—of our great and dear Lombard metropolis—our mother city—with my few pages of explanation. I dedicate it to you on your name-day, and it pleases me to think that some student, in the far-off future, may read your name here and find a memorial of your son's love and veneration for you.

In the summer of 1900, having completed a particularly exhaustive piece of work of cataloguing at the Ambrosiana and having left his library in the perfect shape that his careful conscientious habits demanded, Dr. Ratti started off to cross the Channel on what he called a summer holiday. Enjoying himself in his own quiet way, he toured afoot like any layman, or rode through London streets atop of busses to get the view of the Thames and of St. Paul's. But Sunday claimed the pious priest. He said Mass at Westminster Cathedral. On week-days the librarian spent long hours studying at the British Museum and at the Bodleian at Oxford.

It was at Oxford particularly, renowned seat of Catholic learning, that he experienced what he felt was the persistent pervading influence of his ancient Faith. Recalling its founding by Catholic scholars in the Middle Ages, he felt a just pride in the University's long history as one of the innumerable institutions which dotted the continent and the Isles, attesting to Catholic scholarship for the greater glory of the Church. The names of Roger Bacon and of Cardinal Newman he found indelibly imprinted upon the very walls of Oriel and of Trinity. Strolling at his leisure through the highways and byways of the town, reveling in the atmosphere of centuries of learning and watching the sun gild the towers and turrets of the old mellowed stone, Dr. Ratti rejoiced in yet another evidence of the vitality and robustness of his Faith. For here he found the religious orders which had survived for seven hundred years, alive and flourishing, carrying on in an environment of freedom and tolerance. Capuchins, Jesuits, Benedictines and Dominicans were maintaining themselves in the free atmosphere of a national religion!

It is no wonder that Dr. Ratti's memory of the days spent in England left an indelibly pleasant impression on his mind, whether as guest of the Bishop Casartelli in the industrial area of Salford, or in the more genial atmosphere of the old University of Oxford. It is not surprising that upon his return to Italy the observant generous-hearted priest and librarian expressed his appreciation of English culture with the simple words: "The English reward their scholars with gratitude."

Chapter III

MOUNTAINEERING

ACHILLE RATTI was a born mountaineer. In climbing as a youth the foothills around Desio and the surrounding countryside young Ratti had followed an inner need of his nature. This adventurous urge, common to all boys, found expression in the one sport open to him. For his first impressions were of the distant mountains. They lured and beckoned his awakening spirit. His will to accept challenges was early operative, whether they were challenges to his body or to his mind.

During the holidays at Asso young Achille had widened the range of his boyish adventures at Desio. Here he scaled the Palanzone, the Corni di Canzo and the Faggio di Barni. His inherent love of nature was reinforced by his interest in geology, the study of which he had begun at San Pietro Martire's. When he was professor at San Carlo's he continued his mountain climbing during the summer months and began to receive some recognition as a mountaineer to be reckoned with and to add laurels to the annals of Alpine sportsmanship.

It was while he was librarian of the Ambrosiana that he relieved the studies over the codices and the deciphering of the palimpsests by pursuing his favorite recrea-

tion when the summer months brought freedom to his
restive spirit. Then he would pack up his cassock, and,
clad in his Alpine togs, start off on his mountain hikes.
These he prepared with the utmost care, familiarizing
himself with all the previous records of other Alpinists,
making exact notations of their difficulties and the most
opportune sites for resting and for making observations. For Achille Ratti was always a man of precision
in all that he undertook. He had the most personal and
decided views about mountain climbing, firmly believing that mountains have moods that must not be defied;
that they can be tamed and cajoled if properly under-
stood; and that when the moods of the mountains and
the weather are favorable, they can safely be trusted to
co-operate with the climber.

His reports of his ascents of Monte Rosa and of the
Matterhorn and Mont Blanc, contributed to the *Bolle-
tino* of the Alpine Club and to the *Revista Mensile*, are
thrilling reading. The reader shares the zest of the ad-
venturer and feels his honest pride of achievement in
overcoming the challenging obstacles. He notes, too,
how the mountaineer's caution and prudence do not fail
him in extremity. The admiration the reader experiences
for the precision of procedure gives way to a desire to
share, in so far as in him lies, the elation of a devout
soul and his humility and gratitude in being permitted
to behold those sublime glories on the heights. Achille
Ratti indeed experienced the sense of nearness with the
Creator of the Universe, and his soul was filled with

wonder and worship and that peace that passeth understanding.

During the student years of his youth Don Ratti had
not permitted his devotion to his books to extinguish
his love of nature and the urge for physical prowess. A
healthful harmony was thus maintained between mind
and body that proved fruitful to the development of an
unusually evenly-balanced temperament. This training
may justly be said to exemplify that perfectly adjusted
totality that was the ideal of the classic educators—*Mens
sana in corpore sano.*

When the explorers of Mount Everest started on their
quest, Pius XI (as Dr. Ratti had become) did not
neglect to send them a message as evidence of his un-
forgetting and wistful interest in their undertaking.
"May God, who dwells in the heights, bless your expedition."

Although, with characteristic modesty, Dr. Ratti
makes no reference to the incident in his record, the
English mountaineer, Freshfield, states that he saved the
life of a fellow climber in the ascent of the Glacier
Paradiso (the highest point wholly within Italian territory). "On the glaciers our guide fell into a crevasse and
would have perished had it not been for the presence of
mind, skill, and strength with which Ratti held the rope
and little by little succeeded in drawing him to safety."

. . . . . .

"There are few recreations which are more whole-
some for body and mind, and more to be recommended,
than a little mountain climbing," writes Dr. Ratti suc-

cinctly in his exhilarating and graphic account of his successful feat of blazing a new trail on the eastern, or Italian side, of Monte Rosa.

Although this eastern climb had been successfully accomplished by two Englishmen, Taylor and Pendlebury, in the midsummer of 1872 under the serious hazards of continual avalanches, and three years later by a German, Herr Lendenfeld of Graz, Dr. Ratti felt with his lamented compatriot climber, Damiano Marinelli, of the Florentine section—who fell a victim of an avalanche in 1881 in the couloir that now bears his name—that Monte Rosa was as much an Italian mountain as the Matterhorn is Swiss and that its conquest should be undertaken by Italian mountaineers.

Due mention is made in Dr. Ratti's account of each attempt to tame the mountain from the eastern side—several of them successful—since Marinelli's sad end. In 1886 the Marinelli hut was opened with ceremony. This has since proved a boon for the night—or nights—which must be spent on the mountain, and it provided shelter for the party of four, including Dr. Ratti, who in the month of July, 1889, undertook by a new route to essay the hazardous climb.

By previous arrangement with Professor Luigi Grasselli, also of the Milan section, "dearest of friends and now my old and tried climbing companion," Dr. Ratti wrote to Giuseppi Gadin, the Courmayer guide, asking him to be at Macugnaga by July 28th and promising to join him the following day. Ratti playfully states that he and Grasselli did not reveal their real intention to

Gadin lest the entire expedition should fall through. But Gadin anticipated their motive and replied that he would be at Macugnaga on the 28th and predicted that if the weather permitted they would go up Monte Rosa.

Gadin brought with him a fellow-villager, Alessio Proment, also an able and intelligent guide, who was to act as porter. None of the four men: Ratti, Grasselli, Gadin or Proment, had ever essayed the Dufour Peak (Monte Rosa) which of the Alpine peaks is second only to Mont Blanc; yet Dr. Ratti writes confidently that they knew their men and that the dangers which had been risked heretofore had been due to bad conditions of the weather and of the mountain.

They sought the reassurance that there were no hidden crevasses nor avalanches, and no fresh snow nor verglass on the rocks of the summit. For such conditions are indispensable for such an expedition, which cannot be achieved without hardship, but can be undertaken without real danger, explains Dr. Ratti simply.

The day of their arrival at Macugnaga had been preceded by a heavy squall which crossed the sky from north to south and went off on the Pizzo Bianco side. This meant, explains the author,[1] a drop of temperature and the certainty of the removal of loose stone or serac.

When Monte Rosa revealed itself to Ratti and Grasselli on the road from Venzone to Prequartero it was a picture of entrancing splendor.

[1] *Climbs on Alpine Peaks* by Abate Achille Ratti. Publisher, T. Fisher Unwin, London.

Around us was the fresh grass of the meadows and the woods, above us the canopy of heaven tinged with the most beautiful blue that was ever seen, of a truly crystalline purity and transparency; and in front the Alpine giant, inviting or defying—I hardly know which—with the immense extent of its snow and ice, with the mighty crown of its ten peaks rising to heights of 4000 to 4600 meters and more, sparkling and flaming in the rosy rays of the rising sun.

Here the observant mountaineer departs for a moment to describe the gold mines of Pestarena through which they passed. He notes the precautions the English employers provide for the safety of the miners, praising them for the devices they supplied Italian workmen who are "too often sacrificed to a murderous economy." After leaving Pestarena, Gadin and Proment soon appeared as prearranged.

Gadin had arrived the day before and had left no stone unturned in reconnoitering the route they were to follow. He had climbed with Proment nearly up to the Pedriolo Alp, and had made the entire route to be followed from the Marinelli hut to the Dufour peak.

They reached the hut at seven in the evening after a six-hour climb from Macugnaga where they had visited the solitary little church, and the parish priest (who afterward watched their progress through a telescope until they were lost to view) had given them hospitality. Ratti says he was overcome by a terrible sleepiness just at the wrong time and that he found a few drops of ammonia "a sovereign remedy."

The door of the hut was not securely closed and great banks of ice-encrusted snow blocked their entrance. Cold and tired, they were obliged to cut the ice away before they could gain access. Resting and refreshing themselves with hot bouillon, they went outside to forecast the weather.

Solemn silence reigned around, the stars shone brightly in the infinite azure, almost velvety sky, the huge masses of the mountains and their sublime summits towered in majesty about us, and their gigantic shadows stretched forth and intermingled on the white expanses of snow and ice.

It was eleven at night when they lay down for an all-too-brief sleep, for Gadin called them after a two-hour rest, as they had previously arranged. To obviate the danger of avalanches they had decided to clear the Marinelli couloir by night in spite of the difficulties, before the sun could loosen the serac above as it melted the snow. Although avalanches are not frequent at this hour, Dr. Ratti, aware of the rule, says he himself had heard them active at one o'clock in the morning when he and his brave young friend, Daniele Corsi, had climbed the Pedriolo Alp to the Cima di Jazzi three years previously.

After fortifying themselves once more with their broth and hot wine, they put out the fire, carefully secured the door, and fastened themselves with the rope. Gadin advanced first, tied to Dr. Ratti, then Proment, and last, Grasselli. This was their position throughout the climb. Proment and Gadin carried the lanterns while they were on the rocks. But soon they reached the rim of the famous couloir. This they crossed diagonally, leaping into the snow below after Gadin who had passed his lantern back to Ratti. But the heavy covering of snow buried them up to their waists. They were forced to find more solid footing and this took them out of their course on their way to Imsengrücken looming up before them. Their progress was very much retarded by heaps of light snow, and later by the hardness of the ice which meant that Gadin had to cut steps earlier than they had anticipated. All day, in fact, the toughened, experienced guide painfully cut the path they had to ascend, never once relinquishing the task to the others. Dr. Ratti says in retrospect: "I am still amazed at his muscles of steel and his endurance."

The couloir was found to consist of innumerable small gullies. This made their progress slow and very difficult. Apparently this phenomenon was a peculiar experience to them, for no mention of it occurs in any accounts of previous ascents. And it was for this reason that their crossing was so much more protracted than that of other climbers. They were compelled to go up and down these gullies, losing sight of the lantern before them, while Gadin was continually warning: *Prenez garde, Messieurs, c'est un mauvais pas.* Thus they continued for an interminable time, always fastening their eyes on each step and at each pause gazing eagerly up at the Imsengrücken. This went on for an hour and a half and their progress was scarcely perceptible. The rocks appeared as remote and unattainable as ever. Ratti says his thoughts

frequently turned to poor Marinelli and the grim acci-
dent that caused his death nearby.

"By God's goodwill, we at last laid our hands upon
the rocks and we felt like the shipwrecked mariner of
Dante. . . ."

After a rest and a drink of coffee they continued
climbing as straight as they could up the rocks onto a
narrow ridge between the couloir and the upper glacier.
Suddenly this ridge dropped into a gap which luckily
was covered with a narrow snow arête which bridged the
gap between the rock and glacier. They felt it was perfectly safe to attempt this slender bridge as its width
was no more than the distance between the rope held
by two of the men.

Gadin asked Ratti for the rope and as they waited
breathless, ready to give him assistance, he made the
traverse "with a truly admirable security and sangfroid."

There was a halt of a minute or two, a halt that Don
Ratti found tedious and which caused him to ask Gadin
if he might proceed. Evidently the situation was serious
indeed, for Gadin replied: *Monsieur, je vous en prie, ne
parlez pas; cela me dérange l'esprit.*

Finally they all succeeded in crossing the gap and
were on their way up the glacier between the Zumstein
and the Dufour peaks. They found the glacier smooth
and unbroken and free from crevasses, but this safe condition made their progress slow again for they were
obliged to cut steps in the hard ice all the way. Sometimes climbing straight up, but more often advancing
zigzag, after several hours of silent careful climbing they

halted near the Bergsschrund, "in the shadow of a huge, massive wall of pure ice, whose brow projected and extended above our heads in a regular crystal canopy; a number of icicles hung down like a fringe of enormous diamonds from the outer edge." Here, for the first time, they looked at their watches. It was 1 P.M. They had been climbing for twelve hours with no real halt except the quarter of an hour on the Imsengrücken. "We were entitled to a little rest," says Dr. Ratti drily.

The rocks of the Dufour looked very near. This proved to be one of those optical illusions which so frequently occur on the desert and on high mountains. Indeed, writes our mountaineer:

> The same occurs in the great works of human art; the mountaineer who has seen San Pietro in Vaticano and Bernini's colonnade, both of them so huge, yet so graceful and harmonious, so diverse in their separate parts, yet so easy in their grand simplicity to assemble under the eye in one comprehensive view—that mountaineer knows that here, too, it is ever in the imitation of Nature that our art shows closest kinship with that of God, the first Creator of all beautiful things.

But, such is the power of suggestion, they all felt confident that in a couple of hours they would reach the summit and find much-needed rest in the comfortable beds of the Riffel. With the stoutest of hearts they started off once more, and with admirable prudence they selected a route, not the shortest, but one not overhung with masses of ice and hence not subject to avalanches, as were those exposed to the rays of the sun. Every resource of hand and limb was called upon to climb even a few metres. At this point they seemed to the solitary priest of Macugnaga, gazing anxiously through his telescope, to be stationary for a long time. This route conquered, they cautiously ascended a snow slope which appeared very easy to the climbers. But as they proceeded the rocks receded; the summit arose higher and higher; the ascent became more and more difficult. The stern reality dawned upon them. They suddenly knew they had a long hard climb before them. The snow became lighter and they were no longer walking, but painfully stumbling. Afterwards Gadin admitted to Don Ratti that at this point he almost abandoned hope and seriously considered turning back to look for a place of refuge for the night. At last they reached the rocks! Keen and eager, they pushed on to the summit, for the sun was already sinking to the horizon.

We attacked the rocks by the ridge which runs down right above the Imsengrücken. It is easier to imagine than to describe the means by which we climbed the bare slabs and the masses of reddish gneiss which form the summit.

Suddenly Ratti heard a cry. He turned back and saw Grasselli's axe "flying like an arrow from its bow" down the rocks and dashing off into the snow. There was nothing that could be done and the poor professor was obliged to use his hands on the cold rocks. His gloves were soon torn to shreds, resulting in severe frost bites which it took months to cure. All that evening and the next day he labored under this painful difficulty.

"The giant, being near defeat, began to assail us with his spite and vengeance," writes Dr. Ratti. The wind was violent, blowing off their hats which were replaced by their woolen caps. At last, at 7:30 P.M. they were on the Ostspitze, on the summit of Monte Rosa.

I shall not expend a single word in description of that unforgettable instant, and of what we saw and felt. The memory of such moments speaks with unequalled eloquence to the elect; whereas no words could suffice or even be credible to others.

Monte Rosa is "a double tooth of rock"—the easterly is called Ostspitze, the other the Allerhöchstespitze. They had made the former and reserved the latter for the morrow. The wind had become cruel. They hastened to descend to find a more tolerable position. A projecting rock thirty metres below offered a welcome protection from wind and avalanches, and they proceeded to make themselves as comfortable as they could in a very restricted space. "But," says Dr. Ratti, "it was certainly not as good as the beds and the comforts of the Riffel—for people who had spent the day as we had." While their shelter was perfectly safe, it was so small that no one could take a step in any direction. Sitting down, their feet hung in space; and it was necessary to constantly stamp to keep from freezing. This exercise the place afforded—provided they were careful not to lose their balance.

The cold was so intense that their coffee, wine and eggs were frozen hard, making them unpalatable for either drinking or eating. Of course sleep was out of the question as their precarious foothold would have proved fatal if one of them had moved inadvertently. But, asks this deeply-stirred lover of Nature, "Who could have slept in the face of such a scene as we had before us!"

At that height—in the center of the grandest of all the grand Alpine theatres—in that pure transparent atmosphere, under that sky of deepest blue, lit by a crescent moon and sparkling with stars as far as the eye could reach—in that silence— Enough! [the writer breaks off] I will not try to describe the indescribable.

As they stood there absorbed each in his own thoughts in an awed quietude of spirit too profound to be broken by any word of theirs, the immense silence was suddenly ripped asunder by a mighty thunderclap. The rumbling terror held their awestruck attention as the avalanche rolled down the mountainside, beyond their sight. They knew that it grew in volume as it gathered momentum and mass on its downward destructive course. The reverberations shook the heavens. Again the lines of Dante, the supreme poet of the terrible aspects of nature, came to Dr. Ratti's mind. It came down, he says with un fracasso d'un suon pien di spavento,[2] until it rested on the lower glacier.

Hanging there on their rock they beheld the sun arise . . .

appearing in splendor between the summits—its rays spreading like a fiery mantle over a thousand peaks, and creeping down a thousand slopes of ice and snow, lighting them up with a

[2] A crashing sound full of terror, trans. L.B.-O.

wondrous medley of splendid tints!—It was enough to drive a painter mad . . .

At five o'clock in the morning they left their luggage, and, taking with them only their remaining axes and the rope, they again ascended the Ostspitze. With the greatest caution and after many trials for secure footing, they finally straddled the Ostspitze, and by crossing a narrow gully, reached the Swiss Monte Rosa glacier and came to the stone man of the Dufour Peak. It was 8:20 A.M. They had now reached an altitude of 4600 metres, only 170 metres less than the summit of Mont Blanc. Here they stopped long enough to swallow a little chocolate and to write a short report of the first all-Italian ascent of Monte Rosa, placing it in the bottle which they had found.

Abandoning the usual route on the Swiss side which was temptingly visible and inviting, and much easier than the one that had brought them thither, they returned to their gîte and collected their belongings, hoping to recover the axe on their descent, the loss of which was becoming increasingly painful for Grasselli. Swinging their sacks onto their shoulders, they descended the same route by which they had come, deviating a little to look for the axe. Unsuccessful in their search, they climbed to the Col half-way between Dufour and the Zumstein peaks which they reached at 1 P.M.

Here they found one of the steepest snow slopes that Dr. Ratti ever saw. The wind was icy. They felt no desire to stop and enter into a long discussion as to

procedure. Gadin led the way saying quietly to Dr.
Ratti: *Faites comme moi, Monsieur.* Facing him, the
guide dug his feet into the holes he cut as he proceeded
backward. They all followed suit as if they were climbing
down a ladder for what seemed to the author a very
long time. Finally they reached the rock and soon came
to a deep crevasse. Taking the whole length of the rope,
Gadin first sat down on the slope above the crevasse,
then slid down and finally leaped over the chasm. Each
man followed his example and they all found themselves
buried in the deep snow. By this manoeuvre Gadin
achieved in a few minutes what it would have taken
many hours to accomplish otherwise.

"When we reached the glacier we felt like people
setting foot at last on a broad, comfortable highway,
after wandering on paths of disaster."

Thus they descended the rocks on the Dufour peak
and crossed the pass between Dufour and the Zumstein
peaks, a much shorter route than was ever taken before,
but one far too difficult to be recommended. This was
the first crossing of the Zumsteinjoch, the second highest pass in the Alps.

Not only was their party the first to effect the pass
between Dufour and the Zumstein, but Dr. Ratti writes
without reservation: "As regards our descent of the
rocks of the Dufour peak, there can be no doubt that
it was the first."

In their descent of the Monte Rosa glacier on the
Italian side and the Grenz glacier on the Swiss side,
they became lost. "Ten glaciers have their stately ren-

dezvous in the vast Gorner basin," in what appears to
be "a vast theatre of lifeless nature." Gadin knew there
was a path leading from the Riffelhorn and the Gor-
nergrat to the Riffel hotel; but his eyes were by now
half blinded by the snow and his memory appeared to
fail him.

The sun passed the meridian, and reached the western
horizon, and disappeared—but no path!

"We passed from one glacier to another, we climbed
up the moraine to reconnoitre the rocks of the Riffelhorn—still no path!" Finally it became dark. They relit
their one remaining lantern. They wandered aimlessly
hither and yon in what looked like "a picture of chaos"
but all their searches were fruitless. Proment made a
reconnaissance but it proved of no avail. While they were
in reality only a few rods from the Riffel hotel, they
were obliged to pass another night in the open on the
hard stones of the moraine. Although this was by no
means comfortable, Dr. Ratti says wisely: "It was only
right and reasonable to put a good face upon it," for in
recounting their blessings he says: "We had not met
with a single real danger, not one serious incident had
occurred, not a foot had slipped."

Choosing a place protected from falling rocks from
above, they went to sleep as the lantern flickered out and
Dr. Ratti declares they slept peacefully "to the great
benefit of our limbs which by now were entitled to feel
fatigued."

Later the author of *Climbs on Alpine Peaks* modifies
and explains what he means by "real danger." For

dangers, as he points out, are naturally always present in such hazardous undertakings; but his confidence in the guide, in the conditions of the mountain and the weather, and the quality of the men of the party was such that, barring the unforeseen, there was reasonable certainty that they would come out of the experience unscathed. Yet truth compels him to state that "this expedition is one that does not allow of the least lack of strength or care."

They were awakened by Gadin telling them Proment had found a path a little below them and they must join him at once. So, says the author, "we remounted the glacier and reached the Riffelberg." It was high time, for Gadin's eyes could have stood no more.

At the Riffel they were refreshed with new milk while surrounded by a group who had come to learn of their fate and who were filled with curiosity and wonder. Their non-appearance and delay had created alarm and so, after three-quarters of an hour of rest, they proceeded to Zermatt to soothe the anxieties of their friends who had telegraphed to Macugnaga.

Again Dr. Ratti's praise of Gadin is unqualified, for he generously attributes their safety to his guide's wise precautions which delayed, but did not prevent, their achievement. For no one has ever gone "to and fro, during the same expedition, on the ridge between the Ostspitze and the Allerhöchstespitze, nor am I aware that the rocks of the Dufour peak have ever been descended by others on the Macugnaga side, nor that anyone before us had traversed the Col Zumstein."

With the generosity of a truly great spirit Dr. Ratti gives unlimited credit to Gadin's prudence and foresight for accomplishing this new feat of mountain climbing to be added to the annals of the Alpine Club.

Because Dr. Ratti felt that the opposition which the Marinelli hut had met with abroad was unjustified, he felt it his duty to defend it. It provides, he says, "a vantage near the tracks of the avalanches and enables the climber to watch the enemy at close quarters, and if he should be stirring in the night, to beat a safe and easy retreat, which would be, under those circumstances, not only wise and honorable, but, as I think, a matter of duty." Although he does not feel that the hut assures success to the exclusion of other factors that must be taken into consideration, its advantages, though limited, are not trivial. Anyone who examines the east face of Monte Rosa from the Pedriolo Alp, or goes into the Macugnaga cemetery and sees the grim record of the Alpine dead, knows what dangers lurk there for the imprudent or unprepared, and what may at any time befall even the best prepared, when the avalanches and storms and crevasses exact their frightful toll.

Dr. Ratti, most human of priests and a genuine sportsman, ends his account of the conquest of Monte Rosa with his customary note of humility and reverence:

I am far from attaching to our expedition any importance other or greater than the relative one which it may receive from the goodwill of lovers of high mountains . . . I thank God that He has allowed me to admire at close quarters beauties which are certainly amongst the greatest and grandest in this visible world He has created.

.　　.　　.　　.　　.　　.

It was in the year 1899, in his forty-second year, after he had achieved further fame as a mountaineer by his ascents of the Matterhorn and of Mont Blanc (the descent of the latter by the Dome Glacier being since known as the *Via Ratti*) that the last of Dr. Ratti's climbing adventures was essayed. On the last day of the old year he was passing through Naples. The Neapolitan section of the Alpine Club was organizing an excursion to the crater of Vesuvius. Ratti was invited to represent the Milanese section. It was an exhilarating experience and Dr. Ratti gives a brief report of it in which he tells of the happy dinner party toasting Italian Alpinism which was anticipating the conquest of the North Pole by the Duke of the Abruzzi. Ratti had for a time considered participating in this expedition.

Chapter IV

SUMMONS TO ROME

JUDGED by ordinary standards, Achille Ratti's real career begins late in life. But in the Church promotions come tardily, and advanced age is not of itself a deterrent to fame. There is no compulsory retirement list that forbids or inhibits an older ecclesiastic from achieving renown. True, he is free to lay down his tasks if he finds them too heavy. He may retire to a monastery if he feels that his usefulness is at an end. Thus, Cardinal Rampolla, faithful old secretary and watch-dog of Leo XIII, retired from active service to end his days in cloistered retirement when, after the death of his Papal Chief, Franz Josef's interference with the conclave proceedings directed the cardinals' choice away from him. Rampolla had been the logical popular candidate and had been leading in the scrutinies. The necessary two-thirds vote was, however, diverted thus to a "safe" man, Cardinal Sarto. This interference from the outside can fortunately never occur again, due to the stringent requirements of ecclesiastical privacy which the successful candidate himself (Pius X) proclaimed should henceforth govern all conclave proceedings.

The lives of priests, freed from economic necessity,

made secure by the solicitude of the Church for her sons, are noteworthy for longevity and prolonged youthfulness. So, in Monsignor Ratti's case, it proved no exception that the conditioning of his fame as a world figure came in his fifty-fourth year, when he was called to Rome by Pius X to act as Pro-Prefect of the Vatican Library. Just as, twenty-three years earlier, Father Ratti had gone to Milan to assist Ceriani at the Ambrosiana, so now he was called to the Vaticana to assist Father Ehrle under its brilliant Prefect, Cardinal Gasquet, who indeed had recommended Canon Ratti to His Holiness. This promotion proved to be the first real rung of the ladder to world fame, for it brought the learned Monsignor directly to the attention of the Papacy.

There can be no doubt that it was a wrench from the smooth routine of life in Milan, where associations of more than twenty years' growth had created numerous pleasant ties, and the strong bond of filial affection had been nurtured by daily visits to his mother's home on the Via Nerone, to be suddenly summoned to Rome. He was leaving his beloved library, revitalized by his very life's blood, his "dear metropolis," the Lombard Plain that had bred and hardened him, his connections with the Lombard Church and his "Ambrosians," the social life of the Milanese élite that had brought him many delightful hours of congenial relaxation; and most of all, his beloved mother who with the advancing years was becoming always dearer and "rarer."

The story is told of his farewell visit to Desio, the scene of his childhood dreams and adventures; and of his casual encounter with an old school companion who, like himself, had now become a middle-aged man. They stopped on the roadside and exchanged reminiscent anecdotes of experiences shared forty years before. Ratti's old friend of his boyhood days delivered himself of prophecy, declaring, "Achille, you are going away with the black hat and will return with the red hat. In time, you will wear the white hat!"

The startled scholar's grave features were lit up with one of his fleeting smiles. "That would be a tremendous prophecy," he answered quietly, as he turned to bid a hasty good-by in answer to the church bell's call to vespers.

Arriving at Rome, we can see the carefully-dressed, quiet priest, self-possessed and thoughtful, looking searchingly through his spectacles into the eyes of his new chief, Cardinal Gasquet, the courteous dignitary who welcomed him at the Prefect's office.

Monsignor Ratti knew that his new appointment would in the course of time lead to the Prefecture. But in the meantime he recognized fully all the numerous duties and responsibilities that devolved upon himself; that to justify the faith of Cardinal Gasquet and of the Holy Father, Pius X, he must, on a grander scale, augment the reputation he had made for himself as librarian of the Ambrosiana. Having worked at the Biblioteca Vaticana while he was librarian in Milan, he was perfectly aware of the chaos he must wrestle with and out of which he must bring order and efficiency. Thus began a task, a quarter of a century ago, which he has never quite relinquished, not even during the burdened years of the Papacy's tremendous claims.

Not all Popes have been librarians, and so it is perfectly natural that the precious treasures housed in the most famous library in the world should have presented to Monsignor Ratti's orderly mind a challenge worthy of his administrative achievements. The priceless manuscripts and rare books must have seemed to cry out to him in their neglect to be decently placed in well-ordered arrangement. For not since the seventeenth century had the ever-accumulating wealth of books and manuscripts been properly classified and catalogued.

With that adaptability and forthrightness that have always been so characteristic of him, he went to work with determination and vigor. Carloads of the world's literary masterpieces were daily transferred under his supervision by a corps of workmen, and then carefully arranged in new congenial habitats. All this enormous responsibility of selection and arrangement was Dr. Ratti's. It is extremely doubtful if any other living man could have undertaken this tremendous task with the success and calm assurance of the middle-aged Pro-Prefect. Wherever he worked in silent thoughtfulness, out of confusion came ordered beauty.

Two hundred years older than the Ambrosian, the Vatican Library was founded in the fifteenth century by Pope Nicholas V out of his own private collection of the rarest manuscripts from all over the known literary world. Pope Nicholas intended that the Biblioteca Vaticana should be to pilgrims of learning what the

basilica of St. Peter's was to the religious devotees of
Christendom. With great wisdom and foresight Pope
Nicholas added to the nucleus of his manuscripts all the
earliest editions which were pouring from the newly
invented printing presses of Europe. After the scholarly
Pontiff's death, books were constantly being bought to
augment the library, and a librarian-historian was put in
charge of these inestimable treasures. This ever-increasing inflow of books has never ceased to pour into the
Vatican Library and the task of rearrangement is naturally ceaseless.

Tourists are familiar with the Sala Sistina and the
Borgia Gallery, with the museum rooms, the picture
galleries and the Hall of the Belvedere; but few visitors
who have not serious research to perform have ever seen
the room where Dr. Ratti's desk was placed, the desk
over which he was bent for hours at the solution of
some baffling problem. The Leonine Library where all
the printed books are kept, and the many rooms which
house the reference books and manuscripts are known
only to scholars and visiting clerics. Here may be found
such priceless papers as some letters from Henry VIII
of England, "Defender of the Faith"! and from one
Martin Luther, priest of the Church, who was to shake
Catholicism to its foundations. For it was in the conviction that "the Church has nothing to fear" that
Leo XIII, famed scholar and classicist, threw open the
library to all scholars who might seek out its long hidden
secrets.

What was Monsignor Achille Ratti's life during the

three years of his tenure of office under Father Ehrle, before the Great War created a complete turnover within Vatican circles? Gradually he achieved within the library walls an evolving order that became self-regulatory and established a routine not unlike the old familiar cycle of the hours at the Ambrosiana. Yet how unlike the old life in Milan were the Roman days, in spite of the similarity of pursuits for definite hours! Though the library opened between eight and nine o'clock, there were many hours when the librarian was free to lift his eyes beyond his books and papers, to gaze from his windows down into the Gardens, to reflect upon the imposing history of the Church's glorious past. Largely because of the dreams of the meditating librarian the restored prestige of the Papacy has in our own day become a reality.

Always strongly self-reliant and mentally alive, the Vatican librarian studied the ruined monuments of ancient pre-Christian archeology as he took his daily walks abroad in the late afternoons. Unable to appease his longing for more robust exercise the mountaineer-priest had to satisfy the demands of his vigorous constitution with such restricted exercise as his exacting position permitted.

. . . .

Because of Father Ehrle's indisposition, Pius X, shortly before his sudden death due to the outbreak of the War, sent Dr. Ratti to Oxford to represent the Vatican Library at the celebration of the seventh centenary of the birth of Roger Bacon, held under the auspices of the London Royal Society. On the evening of June 10th a dinner was given the delegates. During the dinner hour, the Monsignor, who was seated as guest of honor at the right of Lord Curzon, the President of the Society, responded to the toast to the representative of the Pope with a brief address in Latin to the assembled distinguished savants, announcing the discovery by Doctors Nogara and Pelzer, of two manuscripts of Roger Bacon in the Vatican Library. The cordial and deferential reply of Lord Curzon was a tribute to one of those scholarly triumphs that must have created a glow of gratitude in the breast of the modest learned librarian.

The three years of librarianship under the Prefect, as Father Ehrle had become, were germinating years that have since fructified with astonishing richness. Living modestly amid the external luxury of faded pomp and circumstance, surrounded by the treasures of countless ages and nations, the Pro-Prefect allowed himself no richer appointments than were the monkish quarters of his cell in Milan. The future held for him the Prefecture —possibly the Cardinal's Hat—though that was conjecture. So the days passed in patient activity and smooth monotony—each tomorrow loomed placid and secure— but by no means startling.

Then came the War! Within three weeks Pius X was dead—the first war victim. Only one act, an act eloquent of his saintly character and noble nature, has immortalized those brief days before he passed on to his predecessors—an act pointing out to his successors what must ever be the Vatican's attitude toward future wars. When poor old Franz Josef, whom the muse of tragedy seemed always to single out for her own, requested the aged peace-loving Pontiff to bless the Austrian armies, the sorrowful old Pope refused, replying in heart-sick accents: "My blessing is for peace and not for war."

Upon the accession of the Cardinal-Archbishop, della Chiesa of Bologna, to the Papal throne as Benedict XV, events in Vatican circles followed each other in rapid succession. Although the new Pontiff was as unlike his predecessor as possible in his antecedents and temperament, being an aristocrat by birth and a diplomat by calling, both pontiffs shared a firm conviction regarding the European cataclysm. Both were pacifists, and earnestly desired that Italy maintain a neutral position between the Allied and Central Powers.

One of Benedict's first acts was to weed out of the personnel of the Vatican all foreigners. In the general housecleaning Father Francis Ehrle was forced to resign. Monsignor Ratti stepped into the Prefecture by this turn of events. For the Holy Father felt an Italian would be a safer man in charge of the important library in wartime. His choice of Monsignor Ratti was also influenced by the fact that he was a fluent linguist as well as an exceptional librarian and profound scholar.

· · · · · ·

From the very beginning of the Great War, Benedict XV, taking up the bitter task laid down by his saintly predecessor, exerted his every effort to halt the headlong plunge of the nations toward self-destruction. On September 8th he asked all Catholics to join him in offering up prayers for peace. An Encyclical followed this invitation on November 1, 1914, exhorting all the nations to desist from their madness and return to the ways of peace. This inaugural Encyclical, *Ad Beatissimi Apostolorum Principis*, was the first of a long series of appeals to the governments involved in mutual slaughter. In it the Head of the Church summed up the causes of the War as an absence of good-will and charity, distrust of authority and hatred of the ruling class; the unbridled cupidity for perishable things. He recalled men's minds to the forgotten principles of the Gospel.

After the rape of Belgium when the Archbishop of Malines, Cardinal Mercier, protested against the outrages his heroic country was suffering, the Pontiff wrote him on December 8, 1914, a letter of sympathetic consolation. In consistory the next month Benedict denounced to the Sacred College violations against the rights of nations. Although no names were mentioned, Cardinal Gasparri made it clear two days later in a letter to the Belgian minister, that the Holy Father referred in his address to the violation of Belgian neutrality.

An appeal to President Wilson followed in April, 1915, in which the Holy Father begged that America do everything in her power to avoid any action that might prolong the war, and back every effort for a hasty peace. The next month Benedict protested in a letter to the Cardinal Dean against the barbarous conduct of the warfare which he stigmatized as contrary to law and humanity. On September of the same year he sadly re-

buked Catholics for condemning their brothers of other
nations.

As an Italian, as well as Supreme Pontiff, Benedict
deplored Italy's entry into the war. In a letter to the
Cardinal Dean, dated the day after Italy's declaration
on the side of the Allies, His Holiness wrote: "The terrible outbreak which has reached even our own beloved
Italy causes us to fear even for her that train of woes
and disasters which usually accompanies every war, even
when it is a successful one."

The danger which he dreaded for Italy caused the
Pope to redouble his efforts for what he considered his
supreme duty: to call the belligerents to peace. His new
appeal was given on July 28, 1915. The war had seen
a year of fluctuating fortune without decisive result.
Words of sublime significance were uttered, couched
in the noblest terms.

The Holy Father recites the litany of woes suffered,
the useless bloodshed, the many tortures inflicted upon
his children. He calls the rulers to task for their slaughter
of his sons. He reminds them that for them also there is
a God.

In the holy name of God [he cries out] in the name of our
Heavenly Father and Lord, through the precious blood of Jesus,
the price of redeemed humanity, we adjure you whom divine
Providence has set over the belligerent nations to put an end
at last to the horrible carnage which has dishonored Europe
for a year . . . It is you who, in the sight of God and man,
bear the terrible responsibility of peace and war. Hearken to
our prayer, hearken to the fatherly voice of the Vicar of the

Supreme and Eternal Judge, to whom you must render account for your public, as for your private acts . . . The manifold riches which God the Creator has lavished upon the lands subject to you enable you to prolong the contest, but at what a price! What of the thousands of young lives which are lost on the battlefields every day? What of the ruin of so many towns and villages, of so many monuments raised by the piety and genius of your ancestors? What of those bitter tears shed day by day in hundreds of homes or at the foot of the altar? Do not all these repeat that the cost of the continued struggle is too great?

The wholesale destruction was incalculable and the greatest obstacle to peace. And what must be the consequences?

Remember [warns the Holy Father] nations do not die; in humiliation and oppression they chafe under the yoke imposed upon them; they prepare for revenge, and pass on from generation to generation the sorrowful heritage of hatred and retaliation.

Benedict besought that the rights and just aspirations of the peoples should be taken into consideration. This he held was the "sole condition of a stable equilibrium in the world and of the prosperous and assured tranquillity of nations." He advised an immediate exchange of views on this matter.

Although the French and Italian radical press pretended they scented a pro-German intention in these noble words (for at the moment it was issued the Germans seemed to have the advantage), yet, on the whole, there was agreement that it was a high-minded appeal. But among the belligerents no move was made to take advantage of this message. Even the plea for a truce of God on Christmas day fell on deaf ears. The fury of the War was unabated.

Italy, hoping to see her national ambitions realized in three months, found herself drawn into a conflict whose end was unpredictable.

After the destruction of the *Lusitania*, another Papal protest was vigorously voiced; but the systematic destruction by submarines continued to take its awful toll.

Since all his efforts to stop the war seemed to bear no fruit, Benedict sought to mitigate its horrors as far as was in his power. *The Provisional Office for Prisoners of War* had been functioning for months before Italy declared war. The exchange of hostages, the notifying of relatives concerning the fate of their beloved ones were undertaken through this office. Without distinction of religion prisoners of war were the objects of the Pope's care. Swiss priests were the agents the Pope used to visit the prison camps in France and Germany.

The government of Italy had from the time of her entrance into the War been suspicious of the Vatican's loyalty. As early as April, 1915, there had been injected into the Pact of London (by Signor Sonnino in collaboration with Signor Salandra) an article defining the conditions of Italy's participation on the side of the Allies. In Article 15 the Allies, as a friendly gesture to the Italian government, pledged themselves not to allow the Pope a hearing if he worked for a negotiated peace.

This unjust and belittling act did not win the applause of Italian Catholics, and even some Liberals felt affronted and expressed their displeasure. It was recognized not only as unfair to the Holy See, but as jeopardizing in advance the cause of a just peace settlement. The one voice that was above national and sectarian interests was throttled. The tragic results of this suicidal policy have been felt in Europe and the world ever since. The wise calm deliberation that was so essential to create a sane social order out of the chaos of the War was absent at Versailles.

Yet, in spite of this affront (due in part to Sonnino's fear of the Roman Question) Benedict continued to work for peace. On August 1, 1917, the Pope issued his famous note to the heads of the warring nations. This note was a peace plan, a seven-point program, which was later embodied in President Wilson's Fourteen Points. The concrete propositions were:

1. Freedom of the seas.
2. Disarmament (gradual reduction).
3. International court of justice (acceptance of the principle of arbitration).
4. Complete restoration of Belgium (guaranteed by Germany, France and England).
5. Regulation of economic counterclaims; reciprocal surrender of claims for costs and damage of the war.
6. Settlement of frontier disputes (especially Austria-Italy and France-Germany).
7. Settlement of Polish, Serbian and other frontier claims, taking into consideration the aspirations of the populations and the good of humanity.

Although Benedict had included in the pontifical note the recognition of Italy's right to claim her natural boundaries, the Italian government ignored the Papal message which the King of England had forwarded to the King of Italy. The obdurate Sonnino in a speech compared the Pope's note to the peace proposals emanating from the German side and even hinted it was inspired by Germany (!) .

The Italian government blamed the Vatican for the terrible defeat of Caporetto, for it was known that the disillusioned troops left the trenches shouting "Down with War! Long live the Pope!"

When finally the hideous nightmare came to an end and the exhausted nations met at the Peace Conference, the Vatican was, due to Article 15 [1] of the Pact of London, excluded from the table, though many efforts were made to have a Papal representative present. Cardinal Dubois of Rouen wrote Gasparri expressing his regret that no Papal envoy was acceptable to the powers. Lord Stanmore replied in the House of Lords:

The Pope is in the same position as a ruler of a neutral state, of which in no case can a representative be permitted into the peace conference except with the consent of all the belligerents.

Never, officially, was the Pope permitted to say a word during the negotiations.

[1] France, Great Britain and Russia undertake to support Italy in so far as she does not permit the representatives of the Holy See to take diplomatic action with regard to the conclusion of peace and the regulation of questions connected with the war.

Before the evil results of the Versailles Treaty began to be glaringly manifest to the slow minds of selfish interests, the Holy Father in an Encyclical, *Pacem Dei Mundus*, in 1920, declared:

The joy which has been brought to us by the conclusion of peace is mixed with numerous and very bitter inquietudes . . . Because if the hostilities have almost ceased everywhere, if indeed certain conventions of peace have been signed, *the germs of inveterate hatred still exist.*

To those who, like the former Kaiser of Germany (with his tongue in his cheek) defended their own sins by asserting that the Holy See should have condemned the war, *ex cathedra*, at its inception, it must be remembered that in 1914 no such Papal order would have received publicity in any of the belligerent countries; and if it might, by a miracle, leak through the censorship of the controlled press, such an order would have been held up to ridicule as the work of an enemy and a defeatist.

For the future of Christianity, in order to save the civilization of the western world from ruin, the policy of the Holy See with new instruments of power at its disposal (the temporal independence of the Vatican, the radio and the airplane) will, it is hoped and believed by many, be exercised in the strong furtherance of international peace.

It came as a surprise to many when it was learned that the quiet scholar Ratti was about to undertake a difficult diplomatic mission to Poland. Subsequent events proved the wisdom of the Holy Father's choice; for, while not actively participating in the policies of Benedict XV, the future Pope, Monsignor Ratti, had been observing, from the vantage ground of the Vatican Household, all that was transpiring, and was thoroughly conversant with His Holiness' aims and purposes. Afterwards it was recalled that the Papal Secretary of State, Cardinal Gasparri, had kept a close watch over the able librarian and had frequently shared with him matters of moment.

So it came about that when the Polish bishops begged the Pope to send a representative to Poland to reorganize the religious life of the country, that keen judge of able lieutenants turned to the Prefect of the Vatican Library. Monsignor Ratti's objection of unworthiness was quickly over-ridden by Benedict with the command: "How soon can you be ready?"

Chapter V

THE PAPAL DIPLOMAT

WHILE Monsignor Ratti was librarian of the Ambrosiana in Milan he reviewed a book describing a diplomatic mission of Monsignor Garampi, Papal Nuncio under Clement IV to the Augsburg Peace Conference, called into being in 1761 to wrestle with the problems that had arisen out of the Seven Years War. This review can be found in the files of the old library in the *Archivio Storico Lombardo;* and it contains a perfect picture of an ideal diplomat of the Holy See. In the light of Monsignor Ratti's mission to Poland and the manner in which he discharged his perplexing and varied duties, it will be seen how the Apostolic Visitor had made the qualities he praises in Garampi his very own. He writes enthusiastically:

A keen and versatile genius, open to any light from wheresoever it might emanate, ever eager to familiarize himself with a situation, despite the ceaseless call of duty . . . His will power was as unfailing as his marvelous acumen. It was characterized by a conscientious sense of duty . . . despite its attendant trials . . . a priestly life of the most exemplary nature, sterling integrity coupled with consummate sagacity, flawless tact, a patient and conciliatory spirit; in short, as one of his friends put it, "He was the perfect model of those ancient apostolic legates whose endeavors have redounded to the honor and well-being of the Church."

Stopping only to visit his old mother in Milan and—as it proved—to bid her a last farewell, Ratti went by way of Munich and Vienna to Berlin. He had left Rome on May 19, 1918, the Day of the Feast of Pentecost. On the 30th, the Feast of Corpus Christi, he reached Warsaw. The Poles were profoundly moved as he passed in procession through the streets, clasping the Monstrance. They felt their resurgence as a nation was being blessed at its inception and their freedom was sanctified and more secure, beset though they were with all kinds of struggles and fears for the future. For, while Russian Poland was restored to its rightful status, Germany and Austria had not yet relinquished their domination in the two provinces of Poland they had held since the partition was sanctioned in 1815 by the Congress of Vienna.

"We can recommend him as a man whose piety, zeal for religion, experience, and knowledge are known to all," Benedict had written to the Polish bishops. And here he was in their very midst! And he had brought with him many tangible evidences of His Holiness' generosity, boxes for Italian prisoners containing comforts from home had been distributed in Germany en route. Immediately upon arrival in Warsaw he handed over to the archbishop the alms sent by the Pope to the poor of Poland.

Ratti's secretary reached him in Warsaw early in June, Don Ermenegildo Pellegrinetti,[1] a former history professor of the Seminary of Lucca, who had been employed in the censorship office in Rome during the War, taking care of the interned men of Slavonic origin. Monsignor Ratti and his secretary made their headquarters in the rectory of St. Alexander's Church. This was their station during their entire stay in the city as guests of the pastor Mgr. Eusebius Brzeziewicz, who was known for his culture and piety.

Many visits were exchanged during the first days in Warsaw. These, Ratti felt, were helpful and important for an understanding of the situations that were to confront him. As in Milan and Rome, his dignified affability and sympathetic tact won the confidence and regard of all. His natural warm understanding and readiness to learn were dignified by the consciousness that he was the Holy Father's delegate. He was soon recognized by his distinguished guests as a worthy representative of the Holy See.

By the middle of July Monsignor Ratti terminated his temporary stay in Warsaw and began his extended travels through Poland with a pilgrimage to Hasna Gora. For centuries from every nook and corner of Poland vast throngs had been accustomed to assemble at this celebrated shrine to pray to the Madonna of Czenstochowa; but since the War the shrine had been neglected. Only a few of the Faithful were kneeling before the Madonna

[1] Later Papal Nuncio to Jugo-Slavia and created a member of the College of Cardinals by Pius XI on December 14, 1937.

when the Monsignor arrived at the Convent of the Pauline Fathers, the guardians of the shrine. After saying Mass, the Visitor entered the convent, welcomed by the Prior and mingling with the friars, conversing with them about their mode of life. Climbing up to the top of the lofty campanile, their distinguished guest looked out from the tower which at night is a beacon light to the Polish nation.

Continuing his journeys, the Visitor went on to Kielce from Czenstochowa. Here Bishop Augustin Losinski was host to him at a dinner attended by seventy priests. Replying to the Rector's happy phrase, *Iam hiems transiit, imber abiit et recessit, flores apparuerunt in terra nostra*, Monsignor Ratti gave expression to a felicitous augury of a smiling and fruitful springtime for the Church and for the Polish nation. During his two-day stay in Kielce, Ratti visited some Italian prisoners in the neighborhood and left a goodly donation with them. On the 19th he returned to Warsaw.

When the train pulled in at the Ostrowiec station a throng of people met him with banners, and all the way from the station to Wlostow, where he was to be the guest of Michael Karski, the crowds knelt along the roadside. "Now I know what the Pope is in the world. I am only a humble librarian—and look at all these crowds kneeling before me because they see the shadow of the Pope behind me!" the Papal Visitor said to his secretary as he wiped his wet eyes.

According to an old Polish tradition, his host Karski

organized a *homagium*—at which all citizens of importance come to pay their homage to an exalted guest.

. . . . . .

On the 8th of September he left to visit the town of Sandominerz, accompanied by troops of peasants on horseback in gay costumes. Here he was met by a delegation bearing bread and salt in traditional fashion. The Bishop Marianus Ryx received him cordially at the Cathedral. Then a great reception was held at the episcopal residence. Everyone of importance was there, including a number of prominent Jews. In a speech, the chief Rabbi of Galicia mentioned that the day was, according to the Jewish calendar, the anniversary of the creation of the world. Monsignor Ratti tactfully replied that it was also a great day in the Christian calendar, the birthday of Mary, who, as a descendant of King David, was one of the glories of the Hebrew race. The rabbi was deeply moved and asked, in the name of the Jewish colony, for the prayers of the Monsignor and for those of the Holy Father.

Here, as in every city he visited, Monsignor Ratti investigated ecclesiastical matters, the condition of the churches, the libraries, and the antiquarian and historical associations. Nothing escaped his penetrating mind and understanding heart.

Ratti's next journey was into Galicia, still under the authority of Austria-Hungary, and hence unofficial in character. Nonetheless in Cracow as the guest of Mgr. Sapieha he spent three very profitable and pleasant days with his charming host, visiting the monuments of the city and perusing the bibliographical treasures.

At Chelm he visited the ground of the old bitter conflict between Uniates who were loyal to the Roman Church and the Russian Orthodox adherents. Passing through Deblin en route to Warsaw, he stopped to say Mass in an Orthodox chapel of the dismantled fortress of Ivangorod, for the garrison stationed there.

For six months Ratti was continuously traveling from place to place, acclaimed by vast crowds of the people, and guest of the distinguished men of the cities.

Because his mission was purely religious in its character, the Apostolic Visitor did not come into close contact with the civil authorities; but on those occasions when contact was unavoidable, there was no attempt to interfere with his work. He was given perfect freedom to send his telegrams in his own cipher in sealed envelopes unopened by the censor. He was permitted to move about freely at a time when that privilege was not granted to anyone else without special permit. Although he had written to the Governor, Prince Leopold, for permission to visit the Ober-Ost region which included the districts of Vilna, Riga and Kovno, he was warned that the time was not propitious. Only two months later he was urged to visit this same territory; but conditions did not permit him to accept the invitation and it was a year and a half before he finally went there—and then under very different circumstances.

Although Benedict had not foreseen that Ratti's mission would extend to more than a few months, rapidly moving events and tremendous changes in Poland made an extended stay desirable. With the collapse of the Western front, the Germans began to evacuate the territory of Russian Poland. On November 14, 1918, Pilsudski established the provisional government. The next month Posnania was also freed from the German hegemony. On the eve of the New Year, Paderewski came to Warsaw, and in collaboration with Pilsudski, achieved a moderate coalition government. The *Sejm*, or constituent assembly, elected Pilsudski President of the Polish Republic in February. Minsk and Vilna fell into the hands of the Poles, wrested from the Bolsheviki. The Ukrainians were driven across the Abrucz, after six months of hard fighting. The new Poland began to function under extreme difficulty. Untrained and inexperienced men tried to steer the ship of state. Monsignor Ratti watched every development with the keenest interest and the most anxious prayers.

.   .   .   .   .   .

In the name of the Holy Father Monsignor Ratti gave the Church's stamp of approval and official recognition to the newly created state. It was then that the government requested that their Apostolic Visitor be made their first Nuncio. This was in March of 1919. On June 19th, he handed his credentials to President Pilsudski. He was at the same time made Archbishop of Lepanto, and was consecrated to this new dignity in the Cathedral of Warsaw. Assisted by notable Monsignori and bishops, the Archbishop of Warsaw officiated at the colorful ceremony in the presence of the President of the Republic, the entire cabinet and the diplomatic corps, all the most prominent citizens and vast throngs of the people. The consecration took on the aspect of a national event.

While the Ministers of Foreign Affairs followed one another in rapid succession, Monsignor Ratti stayed on at Warsaw and was the dean of them all from the point of view of length of service. His uniform kindness and tact won their esteem and veneration, so that, when he left Warsaw, his departure was regretted with heartfelt sorrow. "I must give everyone an opportunity of pouring out all that is in his heart" was his motto as he sacrificed himself, his time and his liberty; for, "I am the first for more than a century to be here as an envoy of the Holy See; it is no more than right that I should give everybody the greatest facilities for seeing and talking with me."

The Holy Father had playfully said to him before he left the Vatican, "You will have hard times—but spend as much as you find necessary, because we are 'poor but proud.' " This advice guided Ratti's mode of life while at Warsaw. Personal simplicity and economy were not permitted to dictate his public appearance as worthily representing the Holy See. His routine of daily duties gives an attractive picture of intimate human interest, told by his secretary, who was closest to him.[2]

Monsignore began his day by saying Mass at seven, or half past seven at the latest, if he had been up late the night before. Immediately after breakfast, he went to work in his office, and gave interviews until one o'clock. Between half past one and

[2] Quoted by Novelli.

two he sat down to lunch with his staff. After this he sometimes, but not often, rested for half an hour; then work and interviews began again. Between six and eight he usually took a walk. Dinner was served at eight; then, after a short time spent in general conversation, he was once more at work—for on account of his readiness to grant interviews, he almost always had writing to do from ten to twelve, or most likely till two in the morning on the days when he was sending off his reports to Rome. These he wrote entirely in his own hand; the archives of the Cardinal Secretary of State contain a mass of autographed letters from him, in a small, neat, characteristic handwriting. In addition to these other occupations he made numerous visits pertaining to his office. Always unwilling to let himself be outdone in courtesy, he acknowledged the smallest service promptly, usually with a note in which his kindness of heart always knew how to find some new pleasant phrase. He used to quote St. Ambrose to the effect that nothing is more urgent than showing gratitude.

The Papal Nuncio's tasks were made very trying and complex by the fact that there were three political legislations reflected in ecclesiastical circles, due to the three regimes, Russian, Prussian and Austrian, that succeeded each other in Poland. The liberty of the Church achieved through the break-up of the three empires was precarious and fraught with enormous difficulties. Certain of the liberal Catholics were clamoring for a new concordat with the government; but Monsignor Ratti, with his accustomed caution and foresight, felt strongly that a secure and stable loyalty should first be created by eliminating the serious contradictions the three ecclesiastical legislations had engendered, thus preparing the ground for a fresh legal status between the Church and the new state. The Holy See bade him nominate an ecclesiastical commission to negotiate with a governmental commission with the object of working out a *modus operandi* for adjusting the status of the Church, for untangling the snarled problems in the various dioceses, and for regulating the disposition of clerical donations. These negotiations were finally under way when the Nuncio had to leave Warsaw.

In order to meet the new religious needs of the changing times, to crystallize the enthusiasm of the Faithful who had for many years been obliged to worship surreptitiously in Russian Poland, and to protect and encourage the numerous convents in Austrian Galicia, Monsignor Ratti was nominated Apostolic Visitor of the Orders and Congregations in Poland. This responsibility kept him constantly on the move so that he was obliged to delegate Monsignor Krynicki, the Auxiliary Bishop of Wloclawek, to co-operate with him and report to him concerning his progress and his achievements.

. . . .

Vilna presented peculiar difficulties, for both Lithuania and Poland claimed the province as their own. The contest between the Lithuanian state with its capital at Kovno, and the new Poland, over this apple of discord, was unyielding and bitter in the extreme. Here was a problem to test the diplomatic skill of the Papal Nuncio of Poland and the Apostolic Visitor of Lithuania, both offices compassed in the person of Monsignor Ratti. He implored the clergy of both states not to become embroiled in the political aspects of the situ-

ation and reminded them that his mission was solely a
religious one. He knew that his every act was watched
and would be interpreted as taking sides in the traditional racial and social animosity between the Poles and
the Lithuanians. Lest his motives should be miscon-
strued, he conducted himself in the most neutral manner possible, even going to the length of refusing to
sponsor certain policies which were commendable in
themselves, but which he felt would be resented by the
other side. So he appointed as Apostolic Administrator
of Poland a man acceptable to the German local authorities and to the Polish bishops, Monsignor Matil-
ewicz, a Lithuanian by birth thoroughly familiar with
Polish conditions and equally at home with the Polish
and Lithuanian languages. Yet this seemingly wise decision was not allowed to pass unchallenged by the nationalistic Poles, once they were rid of the German and
Bolshevik elements.

Monsignor Ratti hastened to visit Vilna when in 1920
he felt the situation demanded his presence there. Traveling in Pilsudski's private train which the President had
put at his disposal, he was met at the station by all the
orders of the city and by the bishops. It was the 24th
of January and bitterly cold, yet the cortège knelt in the
snow before the famous Madonna of Ostrobrama and
prayed aloud. For five days the Papal Nuncio remained
in Vilna, visiting the lovely churches and listening patiently to many contradictory tales, all the while forming his own conclusions.

Directly from Vilna, Ratti went to Kovno, where,

with the thermometer 23 degrees below zero, he spent
two days, interested in the strange aspect of the city
whose street signs are written in Polish, Lithuanian and
Hebrew. Conferences with the bishop and the President
of the Republic gave him added knowledge of conditions. Fortified with this information, he returned to
Warsaw.

.   .   .   .   .   .

The newly created republic of Latvia, carved out of
what had been, under Russian domination, Lithuania,
had begun negotiations with the Holy See. In the spring
of 1920 the Nuncio with his mission started for Riga,
the capital. The party was obliged to traverse Lithuania
en route, due to a broken-down bridge at Vilna. The
mishap brought the mission to Riga, after a delay of two
days at Kovno. Only a third of the population of Latvia
is Catholic, but the Protestants also extended a hearty
welcome to the Nuncio. On the day after their arrival
at Riga, Monsignor Ratti gave an address in Latin to the
throng gathered in the improvised cathedral. The poly-
glot nature of Riga was manifest to the Nuncio when he
listened to his address translated into Polish, German,
Lithuanian and Latvian.

While at Riga, Ratti could not resist the call of the
sea. His passion for nature in her majestic moods, familiar to him as an Alpinist, was fed by the miracle of
the Baltic reflecting the azure of the sky and carrying
the ice floes on its waves to the outlet of the Dvina. Beyond could be seen Courland, wooded and mysterious.

Since he had been appointed Apostolic Visitor of Russia as well as of Poland, the Nuncio made repeated attempts by means of wireless (the only means of communication between Poland and Russia in those days) to be allowed to visit Moscow and Petrograd. For some reason unknown and unexplained to him, his messages were ignored. But in spite of this restriction the Papal Nuncio was able to save the life of Monsignor de Ropp, the Metropolitan of Russia. In unmistakable terms he warned the Soviet government that Monsignor de Ropp was a subject of the Holy Father who was not at war with Russia. The old prelate was exchanged for certain Russian prisoners held in Poland. Through his intervention Ratti brought hope and life to many clerical prisoners.

The condition of affairs in Eastern Galicia was tragic. With the fall of Austria in 1918, the Ruthenians set up a political state which was called the Western Ukrainian Republic. But the Poles of the capital, Lemberg, and of the other cities were in the majority. They drove out the Ruthenians after six months of desperate struggle, completely occupying the territory. The Apostolic Visitor heard hideous tales of outrages from both sides. He was afflicted in spirit to listen to the Polish Roman Catholics and the Ruthenians of the Oriental rite charging inhumanities against each other. He wrote appealing letters to Monsignor Bilczewski of the Roman Church in Lemberg and to Monsignor Szeptycki of the Ruthenians in the same city, begging them to exert themselves to their utmost to end the scandal. Although they each acknowledged his fatherly offices, they sorrowfully answered that their intervention would be unavailing at the time. After the struggle was over, the Nuncio besought the victorious Polish authorities to mitigate their repression of their former enemies. With genuine apostolic fervor for the cause of peace and the Church, Ratti imbued many with a vision of their common Father whom he served. Yet many remained impervious to his high purpose and, blinded by partisan and nationalistic interests, misinterpreted his lofty aims.

. . . . . .

The war between the Soviet Republic and Poland continued unabated after the futile peace negotiations had foundered in a sea of hate. The Poles advanced as far as the Dnieper River and entered Kief in triumph. This temporary success was soon lost when the Russian armies broke through the Dvina sector in the north, following up their advantage by clearing the Dnieper, after a stubbornly fought battle with a terrific loss to the Polish army of men and supplies. The Russians carried all before them as Minsk, Vilna and Grodno fell into their hands on their victorious march to Warsaw.

After a brief visit to Italy (four days in Rome and two in Milan!) following two years of crowded experiences in the Eastern theatre, the Papal Nuncio returned to Warsaw only to be sent to Upper Silesia to undertake his new duties as Ecclesiastical High Commissioner for the Plebiscite. But when he learned the capital was threatened at its gates, he hastened back to Warsaw. Immediately he sent the archives of his Nunciature to Posen in care of Monsignor Farolfi, his new secretary, who had arrived at Warsaw. The government ministers, after forwarding their employees, money and documents of state into the western provinces, held daily conferences at the home of the Nuncio. This tribute to Monsignor Ratti was a recognition of his spiritual leadership in the hour of danger. It was agreed that the legation should leave the city and while the Nuncio made every arrangement in their behalf, he wired to the Pontiff in Rome for permission to stay and share the fate of the remaining clergy and their people when the Bolsheviks should take Warsaw.

But the Holy Father, while praising his Nuncio's noble purpose, bade him follow the government. Yet Monsignor Ratti instructed Prince Sapieha, Minister of Foreign Affairs, that he was to be the last to leave the capital. On the 13th of August the Bolsheviks were only seven miles from Warsaw. A solemn Novena, begun on the 6th, the Feast of the Transfiguration, and lasting until the 15th, the Feast of the Assumption, was spent in prayer and in encouraging the defenders of the city. The diplomatic corps left for Posen on the night of the 13th. The United States Minister, Mr. Gibson, and the Italian and Danish ministers, remained in Warsaw with Monsignor Ratti. General Haller, leader of the volunteers, and General Weygand, whom Marshal Foch had sent to help the Poles hold their capital, both begged the Nuncio for his prayers. Father Skorupka, the brave military chaplain, died while rallying his battalion and prevented the advance lines from wavering. On the Day of the Feast of the Assumption a procession of a hundred thousand paraded the streets while the defenders were fighting off the attackers almost within ear shot. That night the Polish army took the offensive at Lublin and Demblin. The Bolshevik army, which had been at the very gates of the city, began a retreat all along its line. As at the Marne in the early days of the War, what began as a crushing victory, ended in the abandonment of their objective.[3]

The delirium of joy that was felt by the Poles can scarcely be imagined. As the Nuncio had shared with them their anxieties and dangers, their deliverance brought a keen realization of how much his presence had fortified them. This recognition of his services was voiced in the eulogies of the daily press and by Witos, the President of the Council of Ministers, in a Parliamentary speech of gratitude and adulation.

In March of 1920, Monsignor Ratti had taken up the onerous task of Pontifical Commissioner in Upper Silesia as told above. Here, according to the terms of the Treaty of Versailles, a plebiscite was to be held which would determine whether Germany or Poland was to gain control of the great wealth of the mines in that region. The most violent propaganda by both the Polish and German elements kept the Silesian population in a constant state of turmoil. Even the clergy became involved in the nationalistic dispute, and because of Polish dissatisfaction

[3] The 15th of August, the Day of the Feast of the Assumption, is referred to in Poland as "The Miracle of the Vistula" and "The Miracle of the Madonna," just as devout French Catholics refer to "The Miracle of the Marne," when soldiers declared they saw the vision of Jeanne D'Arc in the heavens.

with Cardinal Bertram of Breslau, Warsaw was insistent that Monsignor Ratti be appointed Pontifical Commissioner, believing he would defend their rights at the polls.

As Pontifical Commissioner, the Nuncio left on the eve of Easter, 1920, to canvass the territory and to familiarize himself with conditions. At the Silesian border he was met by an expert of the Interallied Commission who welcomed him in the name of the Commission. The three Commissioners who had approved his appointment met him at Oppeln. They were Colonel Percival, Englishman; General de Marinis, an Italian; and General Le Rond, a Frenchman.

Armed with all the information he could gather, Ratti set off for Rome on the 9th of April, returning to Warsaw at the end of the month. On June 7th, accompanied by Pellegrinetti, he arrived at Oppeln to present his credentials to the Interallied Commission. At this time he briefly stated his object—to create a spirit of good will among the agitated populace. On the succeeding Sunday a letter was read in Polish and German in the parish church in which its author, Monsignor Ratti, made it clear that his concern was to protect the rights of all in a truly Christian spirit, and that the Holy Father recognized all Catholics as his children, regardless of nationality. The newspapers the next day published the Pontifical Commissioner's letter and gave it editorial praise.

Monsignor Ratti made numerous tours of the city, held innumerable conferences and interviews, and wrote his daily reports and correspondence. He paid a second visit to the Bishopric of Breslau on the 17th of June. On the 19th he went down into a coal mine to visit the Shrine of Piekar at Bytom. Since he had been appointed Ecclesiastical Commissioner for the Prussian territory of Marien-Werder and of Allenstein, he felt it imperative to visit those zones of the plebiscite region. The Italian Commisioner, General de Marinis, gave him his auto-mobile and two Italian soldiers as chauffeurs for the tour. On the 22nd of June he reached Marien-Werder, welcomed by the Italian Commissioner, Pavia. After two days at the castle of Marienburg at Frauenberg, he went on to Allenstein. A hasty visit to Warsaw brought him back to Oppeln on the 6th of July. It was then that the news of the Bolshevik advance became so alarming that he hastened back to Warsaw, as described above.

Ratti remained in Warsaw for three months. During his absence in Warsaw, affairs in Upper Silesia became desperate. His presence was needed in both places—Warsaw and Oppeln. Rumors of discontent in Silesia began to reach Rome. Ratti was charged by the Poles with partiality towards the Germans and of being dilatory regarding his duties as Pontifical Commissioner. They even implied that he carried on a surreptitious under-standing with the Germans. On the other hand, the Ger-mans of Silesia claimed that the Poles overestimated the authority of the Commissioner, and were trying to ig-nore the prior authority of their Bishop, Bertram. In such a hostile atmosphere Ratti's every effort took on the color of suspicion and ulterior motives. When Cardinal

Bertram's decree forbidding the clergy from participating in political propaganda (thus eliminating all the priests from taking part in the plebiscite) was issued, the Polish discontent became intense. Although Bertram had acted solely on his own authority, without consulting Monsignor Ratti, nevertheless the Pontifical Commisioner was the object of severe protests in the Polish press.

Those were dark days, days of loneliness of spirit and of deep sorrow, spent in silence and in prayer, the inevitable Gethsemane that every lofty spirit must pass through as a test of faith and patience. What a relief it must have been to his troubled soul to receive a message from Rome in that darkest hour of trial! His Holiness wrote expressing faith in his work and affectionate regard for his Nuncio, tremendously assuaging his wounded spirit.

Eventually the clouds lifted and the light of truth and understanding prevailed once more. Then it was seen how sincerity and single-mindedness of purpose had guided his every act with impartial rectitude toward all. The miasma of war psychology had caused the vision of interested partisans to be blinded by fear and hate. Thus through the fiery furnace of frustrated efforts, great men emerge greater, tempered to grapple with mightier problems. So it proved in the case of the Papal Nuncio of Poland, Monsignor Achille Ratti.

. . . . . .

In March, 1921, news reached Warsaw that Benedict had appointed Monsignor Ratti to the Archbishopric of

Milan, to succeed the lamented Cardinal Ferrari who from 1894 to 1921 had occupied that important See. They had been years of bitter turmoil in Milan, of social, political and religious crises; years of burdensome responsibility and unrelenting labor. The Cardinal's prolonged physical suffering from a malignant disease, aggravated by his distress of spirit at seeing his diocese threatened with disaffection, deprived of younger clergy who might have rendered him much-needed assistance, was brought to an end by death, too long delayed to the sorely afflicted Archbishop.

There was almost unanimous approval in Milan when it was learned that the Pontiff had appointed Monsignor Ratti to succeed Cardinal Ferrari. Great enthusiasm was expressed by those who knew the former librarian of the Ambrosiana. *Popolo d'Italia*, the Milanese newspaper, expressed its satisfaction in terms of warm approval:

His Excellency, Mgr. Achille Ratti, possesses all those singular qualities which render his appointment to the Archbishopric satisfactory to the people of Milan. . . . In assigning Mgr. Ratti to the spiritual jurisdiction of the most important church in Italy, Benedict XV has undoubtedly made a happy choice; for all who know the Archbishop-elect agree he is truly worthy of the high task before him. . . . His world-wide fame as a student of history, and more particularly the experience he has gleaned in helping a new nation shape its destiny under the inspiration of the Church, even when her social and political status was at stake, will undoubtedly stand him in good stead when he sets himself to tackle the problems before him. For in Milan, more than anywhere else, the destiny of the Italian nation is being molded.

Although Monsignor Ratti had not been unaware of the rumors that were circulating about his anticipated appointment to succeed Cardinal Ferrari, when the official word came from Rome, he dictated to his faithful secretary, Pellegrinetti: "At the Pope's command all objections must give way. Had I been asked for my opinion I should have known how to reply." (He had intended suggesting one of his former students at the Theological Seminary for the post: Monsignor Eugene Tosi). "As it is, it now behooves me to answer that I will assume this task under his benediction."

He had hoped to remain in Poland until July, as he earnestly desired to arrange for the pushing forward of the Concordat, intending to go on to Cracow in May to attend a conference of bishops and to bid farewell to the Ruthenian bishops of both the Latin and Oriental Churches. But on May 19th, exactly three years to a day (the Feast of Pentecost) from the time he had left Rome to undertake his unknown and unforeseen duties as Nuncio in the East, he received the call from Rome to depart at once. Three crowded and eventful years lay behind him as the government's private train pulled out of the Warsaw station and the Papal Nuncio, escorted by his faithful host, Monsignor Eusebius Brzeziewicz, and the Cardinal-Archbishop of Warsaw, Monsignor Ladislas Kempinski, bade goodbye to his many friends of Poland—years of disciplined training that seem in retrospect designed by Providence for the hard upward path he was to travel.

In a letter to his friend, the distinguished archeologist, Giacomo Boni, on the eve of his elevation, he wrote:

What shall I say concerning myself? I must say with the good St. Martin: *Non recuso laborem*, albeit the task is now difficult and trying.

I will not, however, allow myself to be overawed by the episcopal appointment or the honor of the cardinalate. By means of the first, the aged Pontiff made good the desire of many loyal friends; and by means of the second, he wished to bestow his sovereign favor both upon the noble and newborn nation and upon my beloved city and church of Milan.

Despite its gravity, this Pontifical decision allows me to enjoy great peace and inspires me with great confidence, inasmuch as there was not the slightest possibility of choice or refusal on my part.

I am entrusted with an arduous task. When one is reduced to mere obedience one feels as though one had the power of two men. And this is only right, both for me and for my chief.[4]

When Benedict bestowed the Red Hat upon Monsignor Ratti, he singled him out from the other two cardinals who were created that same day, June 15, 1921, with words of very special commendation and affectionate regard:

Turning our attention to the second of the new cardinals upon whom we have bestowed the insignia of dignity, we seem to hear a thousand voices emanating from the ranks of the students of diplomatic science. . . . Behold the alumni of the diplomatic school singing the praises of the former Prefect of the Biblioteca Ambrosiana of Milan and that of the Apostolica Vaticana of Rome. His unremitting zeal helped him intensify his studies and deepen his research into the treasures buried in

4 Quoted by Novelli in *Pio XI*.

ancient documents. Behold the students of diplomacy, applauding the Apostolic Nuncio of Poland where, thanks to his firm decisions, wonderful tact and composure, he was able to cement the union between Church and State during the most hazardous moments. We heartily join both sides in their praise of this diplomacy . . . the Red Hat is the highest honor we can bestow on him—an honor which, we trust, will inspire him to assist the Pope in governing the Church over one of whose flocks he is to be the leader. It was to that same diocese that two wonderful souls dedicated their heroic lives—San Carlo Borromeo and Cardinal Ferrari.

To those diocesans from Milan who had come to Rome to witness his consecration, the Cardinal-Archbishop addressed words of sincere affection and high endeavor:

In the name of God we will work together in order to attain those holy aspirations to which my lamented predecessor, Cardinal Ferrari, dedicated his life. Mgr. Calabiana, who consecrated me to the priesthood, used to say: *Ubi Petrus ibi ecclesia mediolanensis*. . . . This is my program: To love you in order to requite your good wishes for my well being . . . to live and die among you. I thank God for being enabled to devote my life to the good of my countrymen; it is an invaluable blessing.

For a full month after his elevation to the cardinalate, the new Archbishop of Milan stayed on in Rome, writing innumerable letters to his diocesans, outlining his work. Cardinal Ratti knew how to combine intimate affection with disciplined authority and these letters all reveal that rare and happy combination so effective for the wisest leadership.

Then, on July 25th the Cardinal-Archbishop went into retreat at the Benedictine Abbey on Monte Cassino where he stayed on another month. Two other letters written at the Abbey to his pastoral charges in Milan are on record. He appeals to their good fortune in being numbered among the "Ambrosians" of whom he is proud to be one. He urges them to maintain their golden heritage unsullied. He recalls to their minds the names of Sts. Ambrose and Charles, and exhorts them to follow in their sainted footsteps; especially in regard to their privilege of educating youth. In a spirit of holy pride he cites the virtues common to "Ambrosians."

There is a feeling of ancient faith and honesty, a golden purity and simplicity, an ever-new goodness always ready to be hospitable; a certain sense of freedom and moderation wedded to a lively intelligence, dogged will power and patience for work, especially in the profession of faith and Catholic and Christian living. It is upon this source that the golden life of our fathers drew for inspiration; that peace of soul; that perfect harmony in public and private administration; the cult of fine arts; the uninterrupted progress of commerce and industry; the abundance of life's necessities; and the inexhaustible treasures of righteousness; and the name which is famous throughout the world of Milan and the Milanese.

The Cardinal declares that his motto as their Bishop shall be the Benedictine *Ora et Labora*. The month spent at the Benedictine Abbey in meditation and preparation for his future duties culminated in a pilgrimage to Lourdes with a group of seven hundred pilgrims who left Rome with the Holy Father's blessing. "I am leaving for Lourdes tomorrow with the hope of obtaining the Virgin's blessing," Cardinal Ratti said to a newspaper reporter on the 28th of August. Here he remained for a week, visiting the famous Grotto of the Apparition, the Basilica and the Calvary. He talked with the Bishop of Lourdes, and while maintaining that reserve characteristic of Catholic prudence, he listened and pondered over the stories of cures that were authenticated by physicians as genuine, and those not yet investigated over a period of sufficient time.

On the evening of the 5th of September he was in his birthplace of Desio. As his car entered the boundaries of outlying Milanese territory, impressed as he was by the beauty of his Lombardy with the Ligurian Apennines lifting gaunt arms to heaven, he alighted and fell on his knees, sobbing and praying.

Stopping overnight at his birthplace so full of tender memories, the next day he proceeded to Milan. The procession, according to immemorial custom, started from the sixteen-centuries-old church of St. Eustorgius and wended its way to the great cathedral where in the beautiful piazza thirty thousand members of Catholic organizations awaited him. Their Archbishop blessed them from the massive doors of the wondrous cathedral. That afternoon he visited the poor of the city at a banquet given them by the Milanese Federation of Catholic Youth. From there he went to the Opera Cardinal Ferrari to bless the foundation stone of the Casa del Popolo.

BOOK II

FULFILMENT

Chapter VI

CARDINAL RATTI IS ELECTED POPE

"THOSE who go abroad," Cardinal Ratti said in his inaugural address to the Milanese populace to whom he had returned as their Archbishop, "see that the Pope is Italy's greatest ornament. Because of him the millions of Catholics scattered over the world direct their view towards Rome as to their second homeland; because of him Rome is the capital of the world. Only by wilfully closing one's eyes can one fail to see how the various countries turn towards the Pope, the prestige and advantages that accrue to Rome from his presence, especially when account is taken of his being *internationally and supernationally acknowledged by all Catholics as their sovereign by virtue of his divine authority.*" (Italics the author's).

So spoke the new Prince of the Church, with assurance and authority. The press of Rome, always ready to pose as the defender of the State's prerogatives, was quick to light upon the word "sovereign." Alarm and disapproval were instantly expressed in political circles. Although the new Cardinal hastened to explain that he referred to *spiritual authority,* the "powerful speech" was not forgotten. They thought they detected a tone of new dignity and a hint of new power unsuspected in the quiet modest librarian.

Although Cardinal Ratti's ministry in his diocese of Milan was of very short duration (five months), the imprint of his personality upon his flock was strongly felt. He proved himself their solicitous shepherd, throwing himself wholeheartedly into his new work with all his customary ardor. Not a day passed in which he did not visit hospitals, schools, clerical and lay institutions, prisons and houses of correction. Each Sunday he went to outlying districts, visiting numberless villages and parishes on his way. His sermons were known to number as many as six and eight a day. His spoken words became eloquent, his address facile and lucid.

Ever zealous to correct abuses and raise the tone of Catholic communities, Cardinal Ratti sent out a pastoral letter from the Lombard Episcopate, which, though it bore the signature of all the bishops of the province, must be attributed to his initiative. The public life of Catholics and the measures suggested to redeem shortcomings that had become a reproach to the Church were handled with consummate skill and had a beneficent effect upon the diocese. Although he made no change in the personnel of his ecclesiastical staff, nor in the Seminary, his personality was impressed upon all that he undertook to remedy. Evidences of social improvement were seen on every hand. The love and admiration of the Milanese for their Archbishop was expressed in their generous response to his appeals for funds to carry on his reforms.

While Cardinal Ratti was fulfilling his duties in the Milan diocese with distinction and promise of vast future good, Benedict XV, the War-Time Pope, whose endeavors to call a mad world back to sanity and peace had proven as futile as they were heroic, passed on to his Maker. The Italian press and indeed the press of all the world outdid itself in eulogies. The anti-Papal *Tribuna* wrote: "Disregarding in his own mind the military and political significance of the war, he endeavored to alleviate its effects in the vast fields of desolation. . . . Under his direction the diplomacy of peace and charity towards distant and even enemy nations" was indiscriminately exercised.

Guglielmo Ferrero, the well-known historian, declared that Benedict's spiritual authority was in no way lessened by his failure to stop the war and to bring peace to humanity.

Neither the wealth of America, nor the Navy of England, nor yet the French Army, nor the promptings of the experts, nor the ruses of diplomats, nor the desire of the people, nor the declarations of the press, nor gold and the confidence of bankers, nor parliamentary sessions, nor the concerted powers, nor the dictatorial craze of the Socialists, have had greater efficacy than the encyclicals of Benedict XV. The spoken word seems to have lost its time-honored power over the minds of men; but this very powerlessness has afflicted the weapons, the wealth, the scientific inventions and the sources of power upon which the modern world puts more stress than on the written or spoken word.

This universal powerlessness is the real terror of our day. (Italics the author's). It is true that the late Pope who, despite his Christian zeal, and the immense authority with which he was invested, although he was successful in alleviating some of the great sufferings of the war, has done little to help restore peace to the stricken world. But then the other potentates could do nothing better. . . .

And yet the bitterest opponents of Papal authority were the first to chide and deride its impotency!

At Milan an imposing ceremony attended by vast throngs of the people and by political and military representatives, was addressed by their Archbishop, who took for his text the appropriate scriptural words: *Erat lucerna lucens et ardens in caliginoso loco.* Speaking in the hushed and moving accents of a stricken son for a loving father, Cardinal Ratti drew a picture of the deceased Pontiff as the unceasing promoter of peace and the magnanimous benefactor of war-ridden nations.

All the world turned instinctively toward Benedict XV to obtain his worthy intervention and have him coöperate with them in pacifying those countries that were at war. Tired as they were of seeing brute force reign supreme, they seemed to be urged towards those lofty and matchless values which they had until then disregarded.

Cardinal Ratti begged all present to join him in prayer and supplication to God that He might give the Church a worthy successor. The evening of the same day, accompanied by his secretary, Don Carlo Gonfalonieri, the Milanese Archbishop left for Rome to attend the conclave. When he bade farewell to the citizens' committee at the station, the tears streamed down his cheeks as he gave them his affectionate blessing.

The hospitality of the Lombard Seminary at Via de Mascherone 58, was extended to him during the days preceding the conclave. Here he must have relived his old student days of forty-two years ago. For the Cardinal, Archbishop Ratti, had reached the age of sixty-five when he was called to attend the conclave which was to elect a new Pontiff over the Church's 400,000,000 souls.

In a letter dated January 28th, he sent to the President of the diocesan board of Milan, Avvocato Luigi Colombo, these words: "Pray and have others pray for our Holy Mother, the Church, and also for me. I cannot express the feeling with which my participation in the coming election inspires me." Was the tremendous responsibility imposed upon himself as one of the electors weighing heavily upon his spirit, or did he have a premonition of his own august destiny?

Cardinal Mercier has left us a description of the emotions that filled his own breast as he entered into conclave on the afternoon of February 2nd, the Day of the Purification of the Blessed Virgin, under whose heavenly protection the cardinals assembled.

We felt that we were under the close protection of the Holy Mother whose image, standing at a few meters' distance from the Sistine Chapel, seemed to watch over the work of the Conclave. A little lamp burnt day and night before the image of the Madonna of Good Counsel. She guided the feet of all those who, that same evening between eight and ten o'clock, came to offer before the Christ of the Tabernacle and to His Mother their final greetings.

Votes began to be cast on the following morning (the 3rd) and the scrutinies were taken until the first day of the next week (the 6th).

Although Leo XIII's *Praedecessoris Nostri* had enjoined absolute secrecy upon conclave proceedings, we have seen how Franz Josef influenced the election of Pius X, (in spite of the Cardinal Dean's warning that no heed be given to the communication) and how it was injected into the solemn assembly of cardinals. Since that interference by a lay power, the Pope (Pius X) whose election resulted from the scandalous occurrence, laid down the most stringent rules for future conclaves, imposing the strictest discipline. In Pius X's Constitutions, *Vacante Sede Apostolica* and *Commissum Nobis*, provisions were imposed for inviolable secrecy. The election of Benedict XV and the election we are considering were conducted under the scrupulous observance of these rules.

It is well to consider the motives that prompted the cardinals to vote as they did in the last Papal election. Fourteen scrutinies, or ballots, were taken before a two-thirds vote was reached. The personal free judgment of each cardinal was bound to determine his vote, although he had been enjoined by the Cardinal Dean to choose a man fitted to assume the staggering task of worthily representing the Church through the storm and stress of times that called for the wisest and holiest leadership. Almost all the nations, weary with the terrible ennui of spiritual desolation after the devastating conflict and the disillusion of the disastrous "peace" had eagerly desired the friendship of the Holy See. Under Benedict they had been sending diplomatic representatives to the Vatican Court. Men's minds seemed to be turning again in the direction of a supreme authority. They seemed to feel instinctively the need of a spiritual anchor. The Vatican was once again the pole-star of the nations. Embassies had been established by several South American countries—notably Brazil, Chile and Peru. Inter-nunciatures were created between the Holy See and Colombia, the Argentine, Uruguay and Venezuela. In Europe Hungary, Czecho-Slovakia, Jugo-Slavia and Rumania were sending representatives to Rome, in addition to those countries which had not withdrawn their legations during the war. Greece, Finland, Esthonia, the Ukraine and Lithuania were negotiating for concordats with the Vatican. Poland's relation with Rome we know was most cordial. Holland and Portugal sent missions. Even England, the four-century-old antagonist of the Vatican, sent a mission to Benedict as far back as 1914, which she still maintains. France resumed her relations with the Holy See.

In Italy a decided improvement in the relationship between the Vatican and the government had been gradually effected. The refusal of the Vatican to listen to the offer of foreign arms to realize her ardent hope for a restoration of her ancient prerogatives, given as a sop by Germany, the hands-off policy of Benedict when Italy irrevocably entered the conflict, had created a favorable impression, even though Mussolini could not forgive Benedict's characterization of the war as "useless slaughter." The defeat at Caporetto was, in the future Duce's eyes, the direct and inevitable result of the Pope's words.

Yet, before he came into power, Mussolini had called the Papacy "the only universal idea" in the world and in words that admit of no ambiguous interpretation he characterized the Church's prestige as unique.

I hereby maintain that the Latin and Imperial tradition of Rome is upheld and kept alive by the torch of Catholicism. If what Mommsen said some twenty-five years ago be true today; to-wit, that at Rome we inherit nothing but a universal idea, then I believe and affirm that the only universal idea which exists at Rome is that which emanates from the Vatican.

Whenever I notice the establishment of a national church I am greatly disappointed; for then I feel that millions of men cease to look in the direction of Italy and Rome. . . . For the spread of Catholicism throughout the world, the increase of four hundred million souls whose vision is riveted to Rome from all parts of the earth, has an interest and a glamour on which we Italians ought to pride ourselves.

In general, at Benedict's death, all things augured a saner and happier understanding between the nations of the world and the Holy See. Taken in relation with the war-time attitude, there was everywhere evidence of a vast change in the temper and trend of international politics.

When we consider all these factors, it seems in retrospect only natural that the cardinals in conclave should have selected as Benedict's successor the man who best exemplified the qualities and virtues that the anxious and propitious times demanded.

"There is a wide-spread opinion among intelligent men that he who will assume the government of the Catholic Church," said the Cardinal Dean to the assembled conclave, "should follow no other path than that blazed by Benedict XV to the glory of Apostolic authority," and he prayed that he who would ascend the throne of Saint Peter should "be possessed of a benign, affectionate and long-suffering charity."

The necessary number of votes did not come until the fourth day after the cardinals entered into conclave. On February 6th, at eleven o'clock in the morning, the fourteenth scrutiny revealed that Cardinal Ratti was the choice of the necessary two-thirds majority.

Stated baldly, the election of a Pope seems a very democratic procedure. Yet the solemnity of the occasion surrounded with the pomp and ancient tradition of centuries of usage renders the scene like nothing else on earth. The sense of tremendous responsibility, the formality of voting, the use of the ancient universal Latin tongue by all the cardinals in conclave, the realization of the impending burden that will rest so heavily upon human shoulders when, as the successor of St. Peter, the new Vicar of Christ shall assume the governance of the Catholic world, the awe-inspiring hush when the Cardinal Dean announces the new Pontiff, fill the Sistine Chapel with swirls of emotional intensity and expectancy.

But let Cardinal Mercier tell the story of the election of Pius XI in his own inimitable manner.

What a spell of deep suspense was that of the election! Alone on his bench, sitting upright, with his head bent down, Cardinal Ratti suddenly gathers himself together. The other cardinals leave their seats and form in threes, in four concentric circles around the elected one. Their deacon lifts up his voice and pronounces, in the name of Christ, the formula: "Dost thou accept the election which designates thee canonically to the Supreme Pontificate?" A silence of humility, awe, faith and confidence, as we had expected, holds us in suspense during two long, very long minutes. Slowly his reply comes in Latin couched in practically the following terms: "That I may not seem to disobey the Divine Will; that I may not appear to be shirking the burden which should fall upon my shoulders; that it may not be said that I have not set a proper value on the wishes of my colleagues; and in spite of my unworthiness which I deeply feel, I accept!"

"Quo modo vis vocari?" (By what name wouldst thou be called?) His voice was completely overcome by emotion. "It was under the Pontificate of Pius IX that I was made a member of the Catholic Church and started my ecclesiastical career. Pius X summoned me to Rome. *Pius is a name of Peace. As I desire to devote my efforts to the peace of the world*, a task of which my predecessor Benedict XV, acquitted himself so creditably, *I choose the name of Pius!*" After a pause he resumed: "I also desire to add another word. I pledge myself before the members of the Sacred College to safeguard and defend all the prerogatives of the Holy See; but it is also my wish that *my first benediction shall be, not only for Rome and Italy, but for the whole Church and the entire world.* I shall give it from the exterior balcony of St. Peter's." (Italics the author's.)

"It would seem," adds the Belgian Cardinal, Mercier, "that the decision concerning the benediction from the outer balcony emanates from the Pope himself."

Outside in the Piazza del Vaticano the vast throng which had patiently waited for three days for the thin wisp of smoke to rise from the chimney on the roof of the Sistine Chapel, was swollen this Monday forenoon to enormous proportions, so that the Royal Guards had their hands full trying to keep them from stampeding the steps of St. Peter's. At 11:35 a thin film of white smoke arose from the chimney. It was a mere wraith, so intangible that it was not certain they had seen aright, or if their imaginations were betraying them. But no! the windows of the Loggia of the Basilica are thrown open and the famous Papal tapestry is spread upon the balustrade. Cardinal Bisleti soon appears accompanied by other dignitaries of the Papal Court. A deep hush comes over the vast crowd below. The splash of the lovely fountains and the cooing of a dove are distinctly heard. Then the voice of Bisleti, the head of the Order of Deacons, announces the ancient ritual.

"*Annuncio vobis gaudium magnum. Habemus Papam, eminentissimum ac reverendissimum Dominum Achillem Ratti . . .*"

The voice is drowned by the wild shouts of the multitude below. Handkerchiefs are frantically waved. Hats are thrown into the air. After a few minutes the Cardinal concludes his announcement:

". . . *qui sibi nomen imposuit Pius Undecimus.*"

Cries of "Viva il Papa! Long live Pius XI! Long live Italy!" are heard amid the general rejoicing. The crowd begins to move toward the Basilica, but the tapestry is still on the balustrade of the Loggia. What is about to happen? The crowd hesitates. They wait, expectant, gazing upwards. Of a sudden the new Pope, Achille Ratti, Pius XI, appears on the Loggia and raises his right arm. He is blessing the Italians on Italian soil! Cries of "It is the Pope! It is the Pope!" resound on every side. Astonishment and a frenzy of emotion overcome the crowd as the troops, the Alpini, the Bersaglieri, the handsome soldiers of Italy, present arms to the Italian Pope, the first Pontiff since 1870 to present himself directly to the people of Italy.

This significant gesture was the first public act of Pius XI. What did it presage? Up above there he stands, blessing the throng of thousands upon thousands with the slow weaving movement of the hand, blessing them as they fall on their knees on the hard cobblestones. Tears stream down the cheeks of the patriotic religious Italians. The whole crowd arises as with a single impulse and cheers and shouts: "*Viva Pio Undecimo! Viva la sedia di San Pietro! Viva l'Italia!*" they cry at the top of their voices.

Even one who has witnessed such a scene more than once cannot do justice to the wild infectious enthusiasm of Italians for their Pontiff.

Soon the giant bells of St. Peter's peal out their brazen clangor to be answered as in echo by all the bells of Rome. The air seems vibrant with the orchestration of the joyous bells!

. . . . . .

Pius XI's comportment upon his elevation to the Papal throne hinted from the outset an energetic reign.

His carriage was easy, erect and confident. He spoke as one having authority. A new spirit of alertness and awareness permeated Vatican circles. His manner indicated that he was his own master. It was as if a strong wind from the Alps had blown through the ancient musty halls, cleansing and invigorating them.

During the first week of his pontificate he gave a reception to the Diplomatic Corps accredited to the Vatican. Replying in French to their congratulatory speeches, he assured them that he would continue his predecessor's policy for ensuring world peace. Although they would have welcomed a statement concerning the Roman Question, he refrained from committing himself, keeping his thoughts prudently hidden beyond the realm of controversy.

Because of the impossibility of the North American cardinals arriving in time to enter into conclave, one of Pius XI's first official acts was to issue a *motu proprio,* extending the period permitted the cardinals for their journey to Rome from ten to fifteen, or at the utmost, to eighteen days. The new Pontiff retained Cardinal Gasparri as Secretary of State and made no changes in the personnel of the Pontifical Court. Father Ehrle, the Bavarian Jesuit, was reinstated in the Vatican Library, and later rewarded with the Red Hat.

All eyes were turned toward Rome and a curious world speculated about the new Pope's policy. Yet, despite the indications that a new regime was about to be inaugurated, it was almost a year before the appearance of Pius' first encyclical. It was felt that Italy and the

Vatican were drawing into closer accord, that the Pope was in reality no longer a prisoner of the Vatican. Rumors were rife that within a short time Pius would appear upon Italian soil—on the very streets of Rome. Reconciliation was in the atmosphere and everyone felt that the new Pontiff would effect a peaceful settlement of the old controversy.

Not only loyal Italians, but many non-Catholic foreigners recognized the need for an impartial tribunal before which all nations might bring their grievances. Disappointed in the futile peacemaking insincerities of Versailles and all the numerous conferences, convinced that no good thing could come out of Geneva, men became intrigued with the old idea of Papal Universality—even men as pro-Protestant as Austen Chamberlain and as radical as H. G. Wells, toyed with the idea. The Roman Question consequently became more than a Catholic issue. It was fraught with the most far-reaching potentialities for peace in a world diseased and torn by war, famine, revolution and economic distress. More and more the Law of Guarantees seemed no solution. It became evident that the Pope, to be the real head of Catholicism, must be freed from all national restrictions. Not an Italian Pope, but a universal Pope, a Pope to whom all mankind might look as the representative of 400,000,000 souls, with whom all nations might maintain relations, was the demand of the times. Pius XI must have been aware of this universal change of attitude toward the Holy See.

But it had ever been Achille Ratti's habit to make

haste slowly. No one was more aware than the new Pope himself that any false move might destroy all hope of future settlement. He knew that undue insistence was fatal to the consummation of his plans. With characteristic caution he walked confidently in the calm assurance that in God's good time the prize would fall into his hand.

The assumption of the Papal tiara had imposed upon the new Pontiff problems of tremendous responsibility. All his gifts of tact and vision were required to meet the challenge of the times. The wisest statesmanship, the utmost caution, the severest patience and disciplined courage were demanded of the Holy Father. The aftermath of the War had brought an economic crisis in Europe that played into the hands of the extremists. The War, said the Socialists, had been brought on against their will. Their numbers increased all over the new map, in spite of the fact that by and large they had, with a few conspicuous exceptions in every nation—Liebknecht and Luxemburg in Germany, Jaurès in France, Lord Morley and Ramsay MacDonald in England, Debs and John Haynes Holmes in the United States and a few others—all forgotten their international principles and allied themselves wholeheartedly with their several nations.

Because they shouted the loudest, and were familiar with the technique of organization, they triumphed over the inarticulate masses who were responsive to their blandishments, forgetting their recent bitter betrayal in their hour of need. In Russia the Bolsheviks had seized power and an orgy of violence against the Church, and the blood bath of the newly dispossessed drowned the voices of the victims of an oppression that even today is not fully appraised and is, indeed, too often condoned by apologists.

Pius XI was eager and ready to enter into communication with all whom he could influence, without, of course, compromising his own position as head of the Catholic Church. A month after his election, Senator de Page, in a silence of respectful attention, read before the General Council of the League of Red Cross Societies at Geneva, Cardinal Gasparri's letter of congratulation, promising Papal support.

The Holy Father is glad to express his ardent personal desire for the success of the labors included in the program of this assembly. *Faithful to the cause of universal peace*, adopted by his Predecessor of happy memory, his Holiness cannot but rejoice at the generous and humane sentiments which have inspired the creation of the second great organization of national Red Cross Societies. . . . The societies, fully aware of the peacemaking office which their traditions invite them to fulfil, have desired to profit by their common ideal to draw nearer together, and to work in common to strengthen the bonds of brotherhood and solidarity between the nations. An effort so generous and so universally praised has been welcomed by no one more than by the Supreme Pontiff.

The General Council responded by thanking the Holy Father and assuring him they would do all within their power to satisfy the needs of the times.

During Benedict's pontificate, there had followed in

rapid succession the numerous conferences of Paris, Washington, San Remo, Cannes, Spa, by the victorious Allied Powers in a vain attempt to bring about the realization of their mutual and separate interests. Finally, it was agreed among them that representatives of all the nations, including Russia and Germany, should be invited to a general conference at Genoa. Many vain hopes and much wishful thinking were pinned to this general conference, in spite of the fact that the preliminary condition of the meeting was the prohibition of any discussion whatsoever of the iniquitous treaties already concluded.

The new Pope was eager to make his influence felt at Genoa. He thanked the Archbishop of Genoa for the prayers he had prescribed for the forthcoming conference and wrote:

If Christian charity ought to reign even amid the clash of arms, in the words of the beautiful Red Cross motto, *Inter arma caritas*, much more should it be so when arms have been laid aside and treaties of peace signed, since international hatred, the unhappy heritage of war, does wrong even to the conquering nations, and lays up a sad future for all. We must not forget that *the best guarantee of peace is not a forest of bayonets, but mutual confidence and friendship.* Moreover, though it has been determined to exclude all discussion, not only of the treaties that have been concluded, but also the reparations imposed, from the scope of the conference, there is no reason to exclude exchanges of opinion which may make the rapid fulfilment of their obligations easier for the conquered, for in the long run this will turn to the advantage of the victors. (Italics the author's.)

Signor Facta, President of the Conference, referred to the Pope's wise words in his opening address.

Under the aegis of the principles of equity, justice, and solidarity between the nations, this conference opens—this conference to which *the Supreme Pontiff, in the fulfilment of his high mission of love and peace,* has addressed august words inspired by a like feeling to all nations, words which are a happy earnest of concord. (Italics the author's.)

Alas! The good seed fell on rocky ground. The conference at Genoa terminated as all the others had ended. No move toward real peace was yet made.

It must have been a relief to his wounded spirit for Pius to turn his attention to preparations for the forthcoming Eucharistic Congress in Rome.

The International Eucharistic Congresses have all been marked with signal success as one who witnessed the proceedings and attended most of the gatherings at St. Mary's by the Lake in Mundelein and the vast Stadium of Chicago, can bear testimony, and who marvelled at the genuine religious fervor of the vast multitudes of believers, and at the missionary activities of the Church, as revealed by the exhibits from all parts of the world at Municipal Pier. Yet, it is said that none of them can compare with that held at Rome in the spring of 1922. It opened in the Court of the Belvedere at the Vatican. Two hundred bishops from every country in Christendom and all the cardinals, who had remained in Rome after the conclave, attended the opening ceremony. The Pope spoke in reply to the opening address of Cardinal Vannutelli. Reflecting no doubt upon the long list of futile conferences, he said with heartfelt earnestness:

It is the avid, not to say, exclusive, quest for earthly goods alone which has embittered men's hearts and aroused mutual hatred. Thus it is that mankind has forsaken Our Lord, *thus it is that mankind has lost peace*. . . . This Jesus you have invited, and He has heard your call. You have come together from all parts of the world, and He has come to meet you. He breaks the silence of the tabernacle. He reappears amongst men, and *peace begins to reign anew, true peace, not a mere image, but the living reality of that peace which the world cannot give*, but which, thank God, can no more be taken from you. (Italics the author's.)

On the following Sunday the procession passed through the streets of Rome. A flight of pigeons announced the signal of the triumphal march from St. John Lateran to Santa Maria Maggiore and the Coliseum, returning again to the Lateran. The cortège was composed of twenty-two cardinals in their red robes, bishops, prelates, seminaries, confraternities, groups of religious orders, Catholic Youth groups, Boy Scouts and men's fraternities, followed by an immense crowd of the Faithful and the curious, caught by the inspiring pageant and the religious enthusiasm. Many tourists and strangers in Rome were so impressed they felt a new era was being ushered in. It is said that one prominent Jewish observer was so moved by the solemn joyous spectacle, that he declared:

It is the greatest event since the war. It is the beginning of
a new epoch. At all the nationalistic conferences we felt that we
were among the ephemeral . . . that buildings were being raised
on sand. . . . Here was the impression of a work of such scope
. . . its foundations reaching into the remote past . . . its future
secure and eternal. Catholicism has resumed all its power and is
today the real master of the world. It alone offers some solid,
organic and concrete hope to the confused and disquieted desires of mankind thrown into tumult by the War. The Church
today is more powerful than she has ever been. We have the
direct feeling that the Pope . . . is above states, sovereigns,
fatherlands . . . in a kind of spiritual effulgence and that all
hatred even has at last faded in his presence.[1]

Great astonishment and wonder was aroused among
the Romans when on a day in April, Albert, King of the
Belgians with his Queen and the Crown Prince, arrived
at the station and were met by the King of Italy attended by military and civil authorities. Stopping only
to pay their respects to the Queen at the Quirinal, they
proceeded to the Vatican from the Belgian Embassy
where five motor cars, flying the Papal flag, met them
and carried them to the Supreme Pontiff, Pius XI. This
extraordinary event was the first intimation of the actual
putting into effect of the veto of Pius IX's prohibition
preventing Catholic sovereigns from visiting the King of
Italy, a veto pronounced by Benedict XV for the furtherance of peace in his Encyclical, *Pacem*, issued in
1920.

This was only the beginning of a series of visits from

[1] *Contemporary Church History* by Orazio M. Premoli, Barnabite.
Burns Oates & Washbourne, London.

sovereigns of states to the King of Italy, for in the autumn the Spanish royal family were received in public audience before the Sacred College and the highest ecclesiastics in the Hall of the Consistory with a ceremony recalling the days of ancient splendor. Later King George V of England and Queen Mary came to Rome to kiss the Fisherman's ring and to receive the Papal benediction. What did these things portend?

The first year of Pius' pontificate was indeed a trying one. More and more he found himself drawn into European politics. Benedict had been accused of pro-German affiliations; and now, because of his espousal of the cause of the peoples in the occupied area, Pius XI was about to be made the target of French criticism. Both France and Germany were putting their cases before the Holy See; for Pius had appointed Monsignor Testa as his envoy to follow events in the Ruhr. But His Holiness did not evade the issue. He said:

I deplore that people of an ancient civilization should exhaust themselves for the moment with still greater potential damage for the whole of Europe and the human race.

Regarding the reparations deadlock, the new Pope declared:

When the debtor gives proof of his sincere desire to arrive at a fair and definite agreement, invoking an impartial judgment on the limits of his capacity to pay, justice and social charity, as well as the personal interests of the creditors, demand that he should not be forced to pay more than he can without entirely exhausting his resources of productivity. Equally, though it be just that the creditors shall have guarantees in accordance with the amount of their debts, we put it to them to consider whether it be necessary to maintain territorial occupation which imposes severe sacrifices on the occupying nation and occupied territories alike, or whether it would not be better to substitute, though gradually, other more suitable and certainly less odious guarantees. . . . Were these peaceful criteria admitted by both sides, the bitterness engendered by the occupation would cease with the final abandonment of the occupation itself, and it would then be possible to reach a really peaceful condition of affairs at which no sacrifice should be considered too great. . . .

Had these wise words been heeded in time, what a different picture of Europe we should have today!

The Papal letter was eagerly seized upon by Germany and flourished before the public as offering the only sane solution to the knotty problem that was plaguing the entire world. France, on the other hand, was obdurate and strongly nationalistic in her demand for a pound of flesh. "Revanche" for the indignities of 1870 still seared the national spirit. England, at the time, was particularly impatient at her former ally's stubborn intransigence. To the entire world France presented an intractable egotism. If it is true, as someone has said, that Hitler was born at Versailles, it is equally true that he was reared and nurtured during the days of France's uncompromising, refractory attitude.

In Pius' mission for the peace of Europe and the world, no country received more careful study than Russia. Conditions there were tragic for the peasants, the economic distress of the cities was extreme, famine ravaged the land, the kulaks were forced to surrender to the local commissars the produce of their farms for Moscow, long queues of women stood all day for a scanty ration of black bread, religion was a crime punishable by imprisonment and death and indiscriminately labelled "the opiate of the people," priests and religious were hounded and persecuted by the new saviors of humanity.

At the ill-starred Genoa Conference the Pope submitted for discussion a memorandum regarding Russia that should guarantee full liberty of conscience for all citizens and foreigners, the exercise of public and private worship to be restored and respected, the property of all religious bodies to be restored. Of course the conference closed without coming to any agreement on these vital matters. Nevertheless, the failure of Pius' attempts to ensure religious freedom to the people of the U. S. S. R. did not prevent him from sending a commission to Russia under Father Edmund A. Walsh, S.J., for the relief of the distressed inhabitants, and the Holy Father himself intervened in behalf of Catholic priests, for the second time saving the lives of many imprisoned clerics.

With a magnanimity worthy of his high station, Pius commanded the mission to proceed with its work of alleviating suffering. Over one hundred and sixty thousand children were saved *in their own land* at this time by the Pontifical mission which was composed of eleven persons: three Jesuits, two Salesians and six laymen. To the amount of two and a half million lire the Supreme Pontiff of Catholicism contributed to the donation collected by the bishops of the Catholic world—an amount most generous considering the depleted finances of the Vatican at that time.

Great Britain's mandate over Palestine, giving to the Zionists a privileged position over all other religious groups, caused Pius XI grave concern. All claims of the various religious bodies in Palestine were, under Article 14 of the Balfour project, placed under the control of a special commission of which Sir Herbert Samuel was the Lord High Commissioner. The Holy Father challenged the right of this commission to dispose of Catholic sanctuaries which had for centuries, even under Turkish rule, been the unquestioned concern of the Catholic Church. In a Papal memorandum it was proposed that the commission be made up of the consuls in the Holy Land of those Powers forming the Council of the League of Nations.

The outcome of the Pope's refusal to acknowledge the Balfour commission was a visit to His Holiness by Sir Herbert in July, 1922.

Many debates in the Houses of Lords and Commons and in the League of Nations culminated in a new Article 14, which stated that

A special commission shall be nominated by the Mandatory Powers to study and define the rights and claims of the various religious communities in Palestine. The mode of nomination, the composition and duties of this Commission shall be submitted for approval to the Council of the League, and the Commission shall not enter upon its functions without the Council's approval.

Although Pius still maintained that the holy places ought to have extra-territorial and extra-national supervision, yet it was a partial triumph for the Holy See that the responsibility for the protection of the holy places should be placed in the hands of the League.

Concerning Italy herself the gravest alarm was felt by the new Pope. In the universal upheaval after the War and the economic distress that followed, the populace was dividing into class factions, and there arose a veritable civil war. Daily acts of violence became the mood of the parties. Extreme Socialism of the Moscow brand was daily gaining adherents. Factories were seized by the workers. Great Britain threatened a blockade of coal without which nothing could function. The government wavered between the demands of those who seemed bent on reproducing all the blessings of Bolshevism and those who sought to salvage what they could of the inherited order. The Pope, watching this sad state of affairs, wrote to his Italian bishops, begging them to take up the cause of peace. One of his letters appeared on October 28, 1922, the very day of the march on Rome, a coup carried out by the section of the Socialist Party that had aided and abetted the entrance of their country into the World War.

In a few weeks after this history-making event, Pius issued his first long-awaited Encyclical, *Ubi arcano Dei*, announced ten days before its appearance by an Allocution which outlined its thesis, *Pax Christi in regno Christi*.

Because the world has determined to do without God it is in chaos, and peace has not yet come. After the terrors of the War, hate still remains, the presage of further wars between the nations; and hence class hatred, hence the misery and famine that are desolating a great part of the civilized world. Like the Jews of old, mankind has said: "Nolumus hunc regnare super nos" and it is paying the penalty. There is but one remedy for these disasters—Let us begin Christ's reign in the world, and the world will have peace.

To achieve this consummation the vigilant and zealous activity of the clergy was essential, he wrote, Catholic activity of the press, the education of the young, resistance to doctrinal disorders of the day, the unity of the Church and the bringing back into the fold of her separated children so that Christ's prayer *Et fiet unum ovile et unus Pastor* might be answered. Signs of such unity seemed to be evident, he believed, when so many governments were seeking to enter into friendly relations with the Holy See in their ardent desire for peace on this earth, of which, alas! Italy was not one.

Italy, our own beloved Italy, does not figure among these nations—Italy, chosen by God to possess the throne of His Vicar on earth; Italy, whose capital, once queen of an empire which, vast though it was, was bounded by definite limits, was destined to become the capital of the whole world as the seat of that divine princedom which, by its very nature overstepping the confines of the nations, embraces all the peoples of the world. The origin and divine nature of this power and the sacred rights of the communities of the faithful scattered over the whole world demand that such a power shall be independent of all human authority and that its independence shall be manifest to all. . . . Italy moreover will never have aught to fear from the Holy See, for the Roman Pontiff, whoever he be, can be actuated only by a desire for peace.

Ubi arcano Dei ends with the fervent prayer that through the co-operation of all men of good will these ends shall come to pass.

Giornale d'Italia gave a very favorable comment on the Pope's first Encyclical.

Outside all party strife, far removed from that wearisome toil which wears men's minds in a perpetual destruction and resurrection, the accents of the Papal encyclical sound serene and calm, and we, who are oppressed by daily necessity and immersed in political passion give ear to the remote appeal and bend our foreheads in silence.

Because he was convinced that ignorance plays so large a rôle in creating the ever-widening gap between mankind and God, Pius encouraged the founding of Catholic universities and watched over their development with ceaseless care. Because God had been driven from the schools of higher learning, the break-down of the moral order was everywhere resulting in crime and disorder. A Catholic university, Pius declared, is a "demonstration of that faith which raises knowledge to the heights, the faith which enlightens science" and it "prepares enlightened leaders for Catholic activity, without whom the organized masses would be a useless force."

. . . . . .

To understand Fascist Italy we must try without prejudice justly to appraise the various influences at work leading up to the acquisition and tenure of power by the leader of the Fascisti, Premier Mussolini. For, as in the olden days it was the proud boast of patriotic Romans to repeat the literal truth that "all roads lead to Rome," so in our own day it is still true that no one can lay claim to true culture who is unacquainted with the wealth of her glorious past or is untouched by the rich heritage of her immortal spirit. Despite portentous changes in her political outlook, reflected in her national spirit, Italy remains today that gracious land, the paradise of poets and painters, the dream of romanticists, the promised land and ultimate goal of Catholic pilgrimage. Because of her persistent universal appeal, the fate of Italy is the concern of all who reverence the genius of her spirit, who value her unique contribution to human civilization, who feel a profound sense of gratitude for the lavish gifts she bestows so magnanimously upon her spiritual children of all lands.

Since it serves no useful purpose to blind our vision, ostrich-wise, in wish fulfilment, let us frankly examine the causes of the phenomenon that puzzles many honest minds of all shades of social opinion and infuriates the extremists among the organized masses and the Communists of all lands with a hatred black as death.

It will be necessary to look behind existing phenomena, to approach the problem with that impartial scientific aloofness that is the despair of the irrational propagandist. For even his fiercest opponents acknowledge that, after the lapse of fifteen years of prophecy indulged in by the Liberals and Socialists of the world, Il Duce continues in power with no visible signs of abatement of his prestige among the vast mass of the Italian people themselves. However much our own press and the press of English-speaking countries generally resent the assumption of what they conceive as a Caesardom firmly established in Europe and threatening to spread from country to country, it is the part of wisdom, surely, to introduce a little reality into the picture and to attempt to diagnose the symptoms that have created a situation which they regard as a social disease.

Taking into account the sunny climate of the Peninsula and the Catholic tradition of her people, their natural aversion and religious antipathy to the class struggle as enunciated by the Communist disciples of Karl Marx, one has yet to penetrate further into the historical factors which make the present set-up possible and even relatively satisfactory to the population by and large. That there are dissident elements in Italy that have never become reconciled to the present regime no traveler with a shred of penetration can fail to recognize. But even among these elements, one soon discovers, there is a deep-seated dread of changing those evils that they have for those they know too well from the examples of Russia, Spain and Mexico. For even the casual observer soon perceives that Catholicism is too deeply rooted into the very fiber of the nation to surrender without a terrific struggle, not only on the part of the Church herself, but even by the least practicing of her wayward children.

"I could wish that Il Duce were immortal!" exclaimed an Italian officer of the King's army to the author. Like so many of his colleagues he had suffered many personal affronts at the hands of ignorant self-

seeking Black Shirt upstarts promoted above their bet-
ters in the army of King Victor Emmanuel. The constant friction and irritation between the two armies of
Italy is evident to anyone who can read involuntary facial
expressions. Yet, since this is not a perfect world, since
one may not choose between an unalloyed good and an
unmitigated evil, but is caught rather between two im-
perfect loyalties, the average soldier of the King, however much he may grumble at indignities that are galling
to his proud spirit, prefers all the disabilities of a humil-
iating position to seeing his Italy engulfed in a flood of
fratricidal blood. For the Italian, unlike his Latin
brother, the Spaniard, remains, in spite of all attempts
to militarize him, gentle and humane; and in his soul,
however obedient to the call of national duty, an-
tipathetic to violence. War is alien to the Italian. He
loves the amenities of the social graces too well. The
adventures of a virile love-life, clean and unperverted,
the quest of beauty and the delights of a cultural appreciation of the things of the spirit, cannot be destroyed
by the business of modern warfare. His heroes in combat
are never bloodthirsty war maniacs; but rather those individuals who, as individuals, risked all to make Italy
immortal. The average Italian soldier would prefer to
negotiate rather than to fight. He is ashamed of the dirt
and muck of modern war. He has no illusions of mili-
taristic glory. He loves to parade in his uniform, but it
is because he knows he cuts a handsome figure. When
Christianity abolished the gladiatorial combat in the

arenas of Italy, nothing like the bull fight took its place.

It is because of this essentially childlike, or *civilized*, quality of his people, that Il Duce fumes and threatens. His attempt to wield a strong nation out of the war-torn and class-divided Italy he inherited from the hands of irreconcilable elements and a supine government, forced him to assume the mien and the overbearing gestures of a Caesar. He deliberately started out to harden the Italian character. All his glorification of war and of the military virtues were inculcated to overcome a certain gentle quality, that in spite of a virile manhood, had disqualified the sons of Italy from competing with the great powers and had kept her a third-rate nation. Feeling cheated out of their promised rights at the peace negotiations, Mussolini, with instinctive psychological insight, emphasized as Italian virtues those very qualities that are conspicuous by their absence in the Italian character. Better to be hated and feared, thought Ill Duce, than to be ignored and snubbed! Thus it appears to the author, at least, that the Italian's bark is infinitely worse than his bite.

With this psychological key to the Italian situation, let us try to unlock the portals of understanding and see if we can appreciate the seemingly paradoxical position of the Papacy toward the present regime. Perhaps we shall be able to fathom the reasons for the existence side by side of the most militaristically organized modern state, and the most splendidly organized force for peace in the world today.

At the outbreak of the War the Catholics of Italy were wholeheartedly in favor of her declaration of neutrality. They never associated themselves with the clamorers for war, either to gain the Allied promise of national advantage, or the bribe of foreign gold. Once Italy had entered, all discussion ceased and Catholics fought side by side with Socialists and anti-clericals.

When at last the evil days were at an end and the victorious Allied Powers met at Paris for peace negotiations, Italy was forgotten and left to pass through a critical period alone. The Spanish influenza carried off almost as many Italians as were lost in the War. The Socialists, profiting by the prevailing discontent, enticed into their ranks many city workers and peasants. Within a few months the country was torn between two governments—the nominal one, and the far more powerful one represented by the trade unions. The Catholics decided to form a political party of their own, similar to the German Center and the Catholic Party of Belgium. The Italian Popular Party was thus brought into being.

While not avowedly a Catholic Party, the Popular Party had at its head Don Luigi Sturzo, a priest. It was the political expression of Pius X's Encyclical *Il fermo proposito*, and was an earnest attempt to save the social order. The first Congress at Bologna in 1919 numbered over nine hundred and fifty branches and had fifty-eight thousand members. At this Congress it was decided that in the approaching elections the Party should have its own candidates. The elections were held in the fall of

1919 and in order that all Catholics might vote, the Sacred Penitentiary declared that the provisions of the former *non expedit* of Pius IX were abrogated. The results were very favorable to the Catholics, for the Popular Party gained one hundred and three seats, although the Socialists had one hundred and thirty-five.

The Popular Party had within its ranks a Right and a Left Wing. The Right Wing demanded independence for the Holy See. The Left Wingers, on the other hand, seemed preoccupied with economic issues. In the hope of gaining adherents from the Socialist ranks, they were making use of the phraseology and methods of the Socialists. In their advocacy of the rights of the workers, some of their members adopted the same violent means that the extremists of the class struggle were demanding. Many priests from peasant and proletarian families came to identify themselves with the Left Wing. Thus a dangerous cleavage among the Catholics was threatening the cause of the Church under the name of Christian Socialism.

To combat this division, Benedict XV had issued a warning in 1920 to those Catholics working in the labor unions to avoid "Socialist intemperance of language," declaring it was their duty to "carry on activities and propaganda thoroughly imbued with the Christian spirit," for, said His Holiness, "it is not by violence and disorder that the cause of truth and justice is defended. The first to be smitten by such weapons are those who use them."

As Socialism grew stronger and bolder in Italy be-

cause of Bolshevist propaganda and the inactivity of the
government, strikes lasting for weeks and months—sometimes for the most trivial causes that might have been
settled amicably between the management and the
workers had they been free to arbitrate—created a serious
stoppage of production, crippling industry and discredit-
ing the country in the eyes of the outside world. Factories were seized by violence by the Russian-inspired
Communists and signs appeared upon their doors,
Fabrica internationale socialista. The railroads were
taken over by the workers and they refused to start before all men wearing the uniform were ejected. Machine
guns in the streets of Florence, Milan and Turin bristled
side by side with cannon ready for action. Red flags
waved from public buildings, and walls were covered
with signs reading *Abasso il Re—Evviva Lenin!* Little of
the Christian influence of the program of the Popular
Party was left in the delirium of undisciplined zealots.
Things went from bad to worse, each succeeding ministry continued to bungle ineffectually. Production suffered from the incompetency of the management of the
workers who found it simpler to seize than to run industry. Deprived of any real government, serious-minded
Italians began to demand order—even at the price of
seizure of power.

·   ·   ·   ·   ·   ·

The War had hardened the Fascisti for the task they
undertook. In November of 1920 the Communal Council of Bologna was the scene of such violence on the part
of the Socialists that Avvocato Giordani, who had lost a

leg in the War, was assassinated; and another lawyer, Colliva, was seriously wounded. This aroused the Fascists to action and their numbers increased overnight until they included nearly the entire population of the city.

The Fascisti were originally all ex-service men who had been Socialists at the beginning of the War which they had heartily espoused, separating themselves from those in the party whom they characterized as *Official Socialists*. Benito Mussolini, the editor of *Avanti*, the Socialist newspaper of Milan, accepted (his enemies say for a price) the editorship of *Popolo d'Italia*. In his new organ he openly backed the cause of the Allies and was enthusiastic for Italy's entry into the War. In his position as editor of *Popolo d'Italia* he sponsored many Socialist aims and was an ardent advocate of anti-clericalism. So intemperate were his editorials that the ecclesiastical authorities of Milan condemned him for blasphemy.

The post-war situation in Italy which we have briefly outlined, provided fertile ground for Mussolini and his followers. The impotency of the government, in the face of the revolution that the Socialists and the Communists were working to achieve, gave a strong leader of Mussolini's calibre his opportunity. The "Official Socialists" did all they could to discredit the part Italy had played in the War. The Fascisti hated the Popular Party no less than they despised the Official Socialists, due partly to their suspected alliance with them and to an inherited hatred of the clericals. Thus the Popular Party had a two-handed contest on its hands and it received no support from the government.

That the Fascists committed many unpardonable acts of violence in their avowed purpose of defending public order there is no gainsaying. Yet, in comparison with what had happened at the hands of Russian dictatorship and was later to characterize the seizure of power by the Nazis of Germany and to drown the Spanish people in fratricidal blood, the revolution of the Fascist dictatorship in Italy was brought into being with relatively little bloodshed.

Fascism meantime grew by leaps and bounds. The inertia of the government and the violence of the Socialists caused many Catholics to believe that it was the solution of the national dilemma. So when the King summoned Mussolini to Rome after the government had handed over power to the military and had declared a state of siege throughout Italy (which order the King refused to sign) most Italian Catholics gave their approval and declared they were satisfied. And when, after the march on Rome, Il Duce, whom the King approved over the heads of the ineffectual ministry, made his first public speech, Catholics felt relieved and secure. For in his inaugural address the new Premier and actual head of the government affirmed that "all religious beliefs will be respected, particularly the dominant creed, Catholicism" and ended with the solemn words: "May God help me to bring my arduous task to a successful conclusion!" Never, during the last half century, had such a prayer been uttered by the President of the Ministry!

. . . . . .

The Catholics of Italy felt more than ever reassured when they saw how Mussolini went out of his way to conciliate them. The public funeral ceremony before the tomb of the Unknown Soldier took on a distinctly religious character. High Mass was celebrated in Santa Maria degli Angeli in the presence of the members of the new government and of the officials of the Quirinal attending the King. Their presence gave confidence to loyal Italians. The King's portrait was placed in the public schools and the crucifix was again fastened to the walls of class rooms and hospital wards.

But the greatest triumph for the Catholics was the proclamation of the philosopher, Giovanni Gentile, whom Mussolini had made Minister of Public Instruction, that the children of Italy must be instructed in the Catholic religion. Although many, both within and without the ranks of the Fascist Party, were critical of the restoration of the cathechism, Gentile was not moved by their arguments but declared that "religion has a formative influence of the first importance on the minds of children and its value cannot be replaced by any other discipline." In April of 1923, Gentile instituted a reform in regard to impartial examinations for public and private school pupils in the middle grades. By this legislation all pupils had to present themselves to the State Commission before examiners who had not taught them, and the diplomas conferred upon the successful candidates were credentials bearing full legal, judicial and professional authority.[2]

Nothing delighted the Catholics more than Il Duce's attitude toward Masonry. He demanded that Masons within the Fascist Party must choose between their allegiance to the party and to Masonry. This break with Masonry, as with an enemy, was a decided triumph for Catholics, for Masonry had been feared and cajoled by the various ministries since the formation of the Italian state in 1870. Since that time the Masons had practically controlled the Educational Ministry. A stormy session of the Fascist Grand Council, lasting three hours, was held on February 13, 1923. It ended with the declaration that "those Fascists who are Masons must choose between their allegiance to the National Fascist Party and to Masonry, since for Fascists there is but one discipline, the discipline of Fascism."

Il Duce was undoubtedly influenced by the most pragmatic of reasons in this new orientation which pleased the Catholics so much, and not at all by the religious considerations that motivated the Catholics within the Popular Party. Still they had to concede that he had accomplished more in twelve months than they had achieved in three years. In spite of the collaboration of

[2] The Ministry of Education, under the control of Freemasons, had exempted public school pupils from final examinations if in their quarterly examinations they had received a 7. The schools had deteriorated in quality and Nasi, head of the ministry which the people had labelled *Minerva nefasta*, admitted he meant to ruin the private schools by this favoritism. While the senators and deputies had upheld these policies so prejudicial to private schools, they secretly sent their own children to the schools and colleges of the Jesuits, Salesians, Barnabites, and so forth.

the Popularists, however, many acts of violence against religious demonstrations were committed by small bands of hotheads among the Fascists. Mussolini, who readily admitted the necessity of a purging within the ranks, publicly deplored these sporadic outbreaks. The popular idea persisted among the Fascists that the Catholic Youth Movement was identified with the Popular Party. Yet Pius XI had repeatedly issued injunctions to the various groups of Catholic Youth to hold themselves aloof from all political activity.

When in the spring of 1923 the Popular Party held its congress in Turin, the Fascists became thoroughly aroused, fearing they did not intend to go along with the new government. Mussolini was demanding that all Popular Party members be excluded from the ministry and that their leader, Don Sturzo, resign his post as Secretary of the Party. In midsummer the earnest, idealistic priest-turned-politician, retired from public life. A strong movement of opposition was again begun by the Popular Party when they openly opposed the Acerbo Law which aimed at creating a solid majority of Fascist representatives in the Chamber of Deputies. When this law was passed, the Popular Party allied themselves with the Socialists in opposition. The deplorable assassination of Matteotti at the connivance of well-known government men did not mend matters among the opposition which hoped to overthrow the ministry.

The Popular Party's alliance with Socialism was condemned by the *Osservatore Romano* and by *Civiltà Cattolica*. This for two reasons: first, because the Encyclical *Il fermo proposito* had permitted Catholics to vote *in order to combat Socialism* which the Church declared was opposed to religion; and second, because if the Socialists should triumph, the whole country would once more be thrown into revolution. In an address to Catholic students, Pope Pius replied to the offense taken at the rebuke contained in the Catholic press by Popular Party members, by saying:

Comparison is made with the collaboration of Catholics and Socialists in other countries. But . . . this is to confuse by lack of proper distinction, facts quite different in their nature. Apart from the difference of the surroundings and their historical, political and religious conditions, *it is one thing to be facing a party which has already reached power, and another to open the way to this party and give it the opportunity of arriving to power.* Why, in the name of Catholic interests, should we give or think ourselves obliged to give, our adhesion to a party whose program involves a neutrality which *per se* would lead to abstraction from Catholicism itself? (Italics the author's.)

Yet, in spite of these sagacious words which reveal a statesmanship equal to that of Mussolini himself, the Popular Party did not heed the Papal dictum. The alliance between them and the Socialists grew more close. The cause of religion in Italy was embarrassed and jeopardized by their continued co-operation with Socialism. When Signor Casalini was assassinated in Rome by Communists on September 12th, Mussolini showed restraint and his attitude toward the Holy See remained unchanged. Many significant acts proved Il Duce's determination to increase Catholic prestige. The next month he restored the cross to the tower of the Capitol, a cross which in 1882 the anti-clericals had torn down and buried in underground vaults.

Pius XI, reading the signs of the new times and bent on fulfilling the Church's mission in modern society, recognized in the new ruler of Italy a medium for the fulfilment of his long-cherished dreams. He bided his time and prepared the ground by study and long consultations with his Secretary of State, the able and forthright Gasparri. From his watch-tower on Vatican Hill Pius XI believed he saw the yearning of the people of Italy for a final solution of the irritating Roman Question. The Pope was convinced that the new leader of Italy's destiny was a providential agent, although a dangerous one, who must be watched with circumspection and approached with infinite tact to achieve his dearly desired goal.

For deeper than his fondest dream of emancipating the Papacy from the incongruous position it held in relation to the Italian state, more passionate than his patriotism as an Italian to free his country from an embarrassing impasse, the Supreme Pontiff of Catholicism was primarily and consumingly concerned about bringing, to a sick and weary world, unity and peace among men. He was not content with signing concordats, though he signed them whenever he could. He saw further into the future. He was patiently preparing the ground and laying the foundation of a policy that should influence future generations. In other words the old Roman Question took on modern implications. It was no longer an end in itself, but a means to that Papal independence that was necessary for the achieving of a holier goal—world peace!

For to realize his dream of the Peace of Christ in the Reign of Christ more than pious phrases and prayers were needed. If ever a Pope believed that faith without works is dead, certainly Pius XI knew it, and he had learned, through his vast experience in dealing with men, that one must not only be as disarming as a dove but as wise as a serpent. He would be constant as a man must ever be who believes in the sacredness of his cause and the grandeur of his vision.

Therefore, for seven busy and crowded years, Pius waited and labored with faith and in prayer. During those years he celebrated Jubilee Year, and gave his wise and earnest attention to the promotion of foreign missions. But in all that he undertook, whether it was the founding of a Catholic university in Milan, succeeded by those at Assisi, at Faro, or the Russian and Czecho-Slovakian universities in Rome, or the creation of new Cardinals, always at the back of his mind and permeating all that he promoted was his aspiration to create counter-forces against war and to bring to pass as a reality the full meaning of his motto, *Pax Christi in regno Christi.*

The Holy Father expressed himself in regard to European and world politics in these pertinent words:

When politics draw near the Altar; then religion, the Church, and the Pope who represents them, have not only the right but the duty to give indications and guidance which Catholics have the right to request and the duty to follow.

For to make the world anew in the spirit of the Peace of Christ in the Kingdom of Christ, mere pacificism, in the sense of passive resistance, is not the method nor the goal of Pius XI. His approach to the problem of world peace has nothing in common with the tactics of the leader of the Indian people, Mahatma Gandhi. True to her tradition, the Church has consistently incorporated new policies and up-to-date equipment to fit her to function in a modern world. Under Pius XI instrumentalities and scientific inventions have been commandeered and put into operation that shall serve the Holy See long after the Pope of Peace has passed on to his Maker.

Chapter VII

THE NEW REGIME

THE Papal Bull of Pius XI, *Anno Santo*, designating Holy Year for 1925, was published, according to custom, on the first day of June of the preceding year. The second reading of the Bull of Proclamation was read by His Holiness in the throne room of the Vatican on Sunday, December 14th, 1924. The document stated that all Catholics who were planning to make the pilgrimage to Rome must come in the spirit of charity and penitence in order to prepare themselves worthily to receive the special graces bestowed in the ensuing Jubilee Year. Then he ordered the junior auditors of the Holy Roman Rota to announce from the loggia of the basilica of St. Peter's, the glad tidings to the people.

The celebration of the Christian Holy Year takes certain of its features from ancient Hebrew and Roman pagan sources. Yet, while observing similar outward forms, the Christian celebration has a deep and unique spiritual significance which was absent from the older ceremonies. Just as a river, fed by streams having their origin in far-away hidden sources changes its character in the confluent stream that broadens and deepens as it flows along on its predestined course to the sea, so rites of the Christian religion have acquired new spiritual meanings when adapted from the ceremonies of religions of the past.

In memory of the Hebrews' deliverance from slavery in Egypt and their conquest of Canaan, the Lord commanded Moses to set apart every seventh and fifteenth year that the people and the land might rest. Thus the Hebrew Holy Year had a politico-economic foundation.

The ancient Romans celebrated every hundredth year with games and ceremonies in honor of the gods, when youths and maidens sang an invocation to Apollo, the god of Light. "O see that nothing may behold you mightier than Rome," [1] they chanted.

Pope Boniface VIII gained the inspiration of Holy Year from these Biblical and pagan sources. The sacred pilgrimage to the tomb of the Apostle Peter, when, without bidding, multitudes came to Rome on New Year's eve, 1300, to commemorate the new century in accordance with what appeared to be an ancient tradition, formed the origin of the institution of Holy Year. Thrilled by the spectacle of this spontaneous foregathering of the Faithful, Pope Boniface wrote his Bull of Jubilee. This proclaimed to the Catholic world a year of Jubilee to be celebrated every hundred years.

Clement VI reduced the time to fifty years; Urban VI to thirty-three, and finally Paul II to twenty-five years. Clement VI in 1350 added to the pilgrimage to St. Peter's one to the basilica of St. John Lateran, and Gregory XI that of Santa Maria Maggiore.

[1] *Carmen Seculare* of Horace.

Catholicism has always held in veneration the ancient churches of Rome. In many cases these have arisen upon the ruins of pagan temples—as the old church, Santa Maria sopra Minerva, testifies. The catacombs containing the sacred bones of the early Christian martyrs have always been the goal of pilgrimage for the Faithful. A sense of dedication and a renewal of Christian fervor brought the devout to the Eternal City to be shriven and fortified in their Faith.

A few days prior to the opening of the Holy Door, at the 1925 Jubilee Year, the customary gifts of a golden hammer, a golden basin and a commemorative medal were presented to His Holiness, Pope Pius XI. Before the actual opening of the Holy Door the officials of the *Reverenda Fabrica di San Pietro* removed all the medals locked in a small leaden casket, where they had been walled up in the Door from previous ceremonies, and carried these to the Pope. What strange emotions must have filled the breast of the Pontiff beholding these symbols touched by the hands of his departed predecessors!

The ceremony of opening the Holy Door was brief but impressive. The Supreme Pontiff, followed by his court, descended to the atrium of the basilica. Representatives of the regular clergy, wearing their appropriate insignia, lined up along the corridors and staircases of the Apostolic Palace; representatives of the lesser basilicas and of the collegiate churches waited apart for the Holy Father's arrival. Attired in the falda, cammice, alb, girdle and cope, and wearing on his head the precious mitre, Pius descended to the portico of the

Vatican basilica. Near the statue of Constantine at the foot of the Scala Regia, he ascended the *sedia gestatoria*, bearing in his hand a lighted candle and flanked by the famous flabella. The notes of the silver trumpets sounded forth, as at all Papal functions, and the effect was splendidly impressive.

Arriving at the left of the Holy Door, His Holiness mounted his throne as the *Veni Creator* was sung. Passing the lighted taper to the Grand Penitentiary, Pius ascended the steps of the Holy Door and delivered a blow with the hammer, intoning in Latin: "Open to me the Gates of Justice," to which the cantors responded: "Entering therein, I shall confess to the Lord." At a second blow of the hammer, the Pope intoned: "I will enter Thy House, O Lord," the cantors replying: "I will adore Thee in Thy Holy Temple." At the third blow came the Papal words: "Open to me the Gates, since God is with us," to which the cantors responded: "Who hath wrought power in Israel." At the third blow the Door fell. Returning to his Throne, the Holy Father intoned: "O Lord, hear my prayer," as he invoked God's blessing. He continued: "This is the Door of the Lord, the just shall enter therein," after which he took the lighted taper and approached the open portal. At the threshold he knelt bareheaded and intoned a *Te Deum*, while the angelic Sistine Choir took up the glorious refrain on waves of solemn sound. His Holiness then proceeded to the Chapel of the Pietà, as the clergy, regular and secular, entered through the open door, passing on into the Basilica.

The seniors of the confraternities who have charge of all the ceremonies of Jubilee Year, were then presented to the Holy Father who addressed them on the dignity of their office. The Pope then gave his blessing to all the Faithful who were attending and to all the Catholic associations and societies present with their respective banners. His Holiness then departed in solemn procession to the Gregorian Chapel and returned to his private apartments. Thus ended the inauguration of Holy Year.

Innumerable picturesque and historic ceremonies took place during Holy Year in the third year of the pontificate of Pius XI. None was more beautiful than that of the *Giovani Cattolichi* which began at the tomb of the boy-martyr, St. Pancratius, where the lads took a solemn oath. They then visited the Seven Churches in accordance with the instructions of St. Philip Neri, who sought to combine for the youth of his day pious devotion with healthful exercise. The youngsters started from St. Peter's and went to San Paolo fuori le Mura and on to St. Sebastian's. At the luncheon served at the Villa Celimontana the boys heard a layman tell of the thrilling life of St. Philip. Then they went on to the road again to St. John Lateran, the Cathedral Church of Rome, and from there to Santa Croce in Gerusalemme, ending with visits to San Lorenzo fuori le Mura and to Santa Maria Maggiore, where a distinguished preacher addressed them and the celebration was concluded with a *Te Deum* and a Benediction.

On Christmas Eve Pius XI closed the Holy Door with ceremony. A few days later his major domo replaced the medals of gold, silver and bronze in the leaden casket, including the new one struck for Holy Year, 1925, in the vaults below the threshold. For another quarter of a century the Holy Door remains sealed until a pontiff other than Pius XI shall again summon the Faithful to Rome for a new Jubilee. Yet the memory of Holy Year, 1925, must remain fresh and inspiring to our most human of popes whose pontificate has been marked by so many thrilling experiences. For Pius XI was brought into direct personal contact with a quarter of a million of his flock. Coming from the uttermost parts of the earth and speaking every tongue under heaven, they converged upon the Eternal City and knelt at the tomb of the Apostle Peter whom Pius XI succeeds as the Vicar of Christ.

．　　．　　．　　．　　．　　．

In Rome, during Holy Year, over a million Catholics were given concrete proof of how the Church is conducting herself in the mission field. The great Missionary Exposition was a panorama of missionary endeavor, the results of which Pius XI wished to demonstrate to the people—not only in its religious significance but also in its social benefits to the natives and to the entire outside world. This wonderful exhibit is now permanently housed at the Lateran beside the Pagan and Christian Antiquarian Museum and is known as the Ethnological Missionary Museum.

No pontiff of Rome has taken with more literal seriousness the august command of Christ to his apostles to go into all the world and preach the gospel than has

Pius XI, translating that injunction in terms of incessant labor and watchful solicitude over the vast reaches of Catholic missionary endeavor. Under his aegis the Catholic Church has increased by almost one-third its missionary field. Pius' enthusiasm for missionary labor has never flagged. Those nearest to him are amazed at the unsparing energy he has expended upon the evangelization of the world.

It was on May 3, 1933, that Pius issued a *motu proprio*, ordering the removal from France to Rome of the organization for the Propagation of the Faith. This move was in keeping with the original intention of its founder, Pauline Jaricot of Lyons, who during her lifetime expressed the desire that the distribution of the funds collected by the Council should be made in Rome where they might be impartially allotted by the organization most familiar with the needs of each mission.

Under this wise arrangement new life was infused into the hundred-year-old organization. In its commodious building in Rome the general council now meets each month. The budget for the relief of missions is allotted each March and on this occasion all foreign members are expected to be present. In spite of the world depression its receipts amounted to fifty-one million lire in 1931. Since Pius XI's accession to the Papacy in 1922 over four hundred and sixty million Italian lire have been collected. The interest on the untouched principal of the financial settlement by the Italian state due the Vatican under the Law of Guarantees goes to support the work of the missions.

The Association of the Holy Childhood which Pius co-ordinated by a *motu proprio* of 1929 with the Society of St. Peter the Apostle and with the Society of the Propagation, has saved twenty million abandoned children and takes care of half a million annually.

The purely spiritual aspect of missionary labor is stressed by Pius. It must not "become a contact between savages and adventurous missioners." The immediate result of the centralizing policy of the Pontiff has been to knit the Chinese, African and Japanese churches more closely to the Holy See, and by so doing, to create far greater regional liberty.

Pius XI's missionary policies are determined by local conditions and by the times. A rare insight into the needs of native peoples and delicate spiritual tact have given a finesse to missionary endeavor that could only have originated in the mind and heart of a spirit completely liberated from the narrow prejudices that have too often dictated the activities of proselytizers. His policy of promoting seminaries for the preparation of native clergy has resulted in an ever-increasing number of African and Asiatic priests. The supernational character of the Church is not only a tenet of faith but an actual practicing reality. Not from governments, but from Christ Himself, does the missioner's sublime vocation originate. Pius declared to bishops of China that the Church, even in the face of governmental and political interference, has affectionately assisted native peoples to whom it preaches the Gospel.

The Church always opposes among its ministers any worldly influence or nationalistic spirit. But above all it opposes these things among those sent in its name to preach the Gospel in foreign lands. It has always claimed the right to preach the gospel without political interference. *It has never permitted its missions to be used as a political instrument by earthly powers.*[2] (Italics the author's.)

In his Encyclical, *Rerum Ecclesiae*, issued in 1926, Pius urged the increase of native clergy; and believing they are best fitted to know the needs of their own people, he emphasized that they should be given responsibility in their own dioceses as soon as possible. This policy has the advantage, in times of political disturbance and war, of freeing the Church from suspicion of ulterior nationalistic motives. He therefore tells the European missionaries that they are only pioneers who must relinquish their posts as soon as the native clergy are trained to assume the work.

Especially does the present Pontiff lay upon European priests the injunction that they must not hold the thought that "natives are of an inferior race and of obtuse intelligence." He boldly asserts that the extreme slowness of mind of peoples in barbarian lands is to be attributed to the condition of their lives and that "experience has shown that the natives of the remote regions of the East and of the South can hold their own with European races." His wisdom and humanity are

[2] The falsity of the recent malicious canard in certain New York newspapers purporting inside knowledge of the Holy See's backing of Japan in her aggression in China was known by well-informed persons to be contrary to practice and fact before it was officially denied. L.B.-O.

shown in his insistence that missions shall not be concentrated in large centers but must be scattered as widely as possible in outlying districts. Here they must heal the sick and nurture the children, instruct the poorer natives in agriculture, industry and the arts—not neglecting the more prosperous. Costly buildings must be deferred until such time as they are demanded by the natives. Not until the missionaries are native citizens can the Holy See feel assured that the Faith is permanently implanted in the soil of foreign lands.

On October 28, 1926, Pius XI consecrated with his own hands six native Chinese bishops. There are today more than twelve native bishops. Half of the clergy are Chinese and members of the religious orders are natives. There are fifty missionary districts and twelve thousand five hundred churches and chapels to minister to the two million six hundred thousand converts. Churches and church schools are built in the native style of architecture, by order of the Pope.

These innovations in the missionary activity of the Catholic Church in China are cited as typical in all other fields and have resulted in so favorable a change of native sentiment toward Catholic missions that, in spite of the chaos and political confusion of our day and despite some local persecutions, Catholic missionaries have stayed at their posts. Even today (September, 1937) the Maryknoll Sisters, staffing the Mercy Hospital in a Shanghai suburb, do not abandon their station despite violent warfare. The din of bursting shells, machine-gun fire, bombs and airplane raids, cause the

Sisters grave concern as their patients are mental cases and their sufferings are aggravated by the terrific noise and the acute danger.

Pius XI's missionary policy has been conducted not only to make converts in foreign lands, but *to implant Christ permanently* in the far reaches of the globe. Only so can the Kingdom of Christ become a reality on this earth which, through the invention of the radio and the airplane, has so shrunken in size that no section, however remote, can be influenced for good or ill without affecting the entire civilized world.

.   .   .   .   .   .

In retrospect it seems almost as though Providence, whose ways are hid in mystery, had brought together two extraordinary men, Pope Pius XI and Signor Mussolini, to act as his agents in bringing about that consummation which for sixty years thousands of loyal Italians and millions of Catholics scattered all over the globe have prayed for—reconciliation between the Italian State and the Holy See. While Il Duce is by no means what is called "a good Catholic," he yet has regarded the Church as his country's chief ornament and a powerful instrument for the fulfilment of Italy's future greatness. And while Pius has seen in Mussolini a man whose methods he could often not countenance as Pope and Shepherd of souls, yet he has not been blind to the new era of prosperity and order which Mussolini has inaugurated. As Pius discovered that Il Duce did not intend to interfere with the Church's prerogatives, he began to hope that the first overtures toward an understanding might be prepared. For thirty months he and his Secretary of State, the canny Gasparri, were in constant contact in the working out of the Roman Question. And as soon as Mussolini grew aware that the Vatican was not trying to stop his progress, he gave frequent evidence of his friendliness and appreciation of what amounted to tacit recognition.

Already in the Chamber of Deputies Il Duce had dumbfounded the Assembly by the sweeping categoric statement he uttered about what should be the relationship between the Fascist State and the Catholic Church.

There is a problem to which I wish to call the attention of the Party's representatives. This problem is the possibility of relations, not merely between us Fascists and the Catholic Party, but between Italy and the Vatican.

From the age of fifteen to twenty-five we have all drunk at the spring of anti-clericalism; we have all hated the cruel old Vatican She-wolf of which Carducci spoke, if I am not mistaken, in his ode to Ferrara; we have all heard of a "sinister Pontiff" as opposed to the august soothsayer of the Truth, and about the "black-haired woman of the Tiber" who pointed out a nameless heap of ruins to the pilgrims who ventured toward St. Peter's.

But all these things which are most brilliant in literature, are anachronistic, to say the least, as far as we unprejudiced Fascists are concerned.

I maintain that the imperial Latin traditions of Rome are represented today by Catholicism.

How can a nation be strong in adversity and great in victory if it gives itself up to the fallacious hedonism of selfish appetites and fails to translate its patriotism in terms of the absolute: GOD?

The imperial strength of Catholic, universal Rome, of which Christ [3] and St. Paul proclaimed themselves citizens, is a factor of our national unity which we cannot afford to disregard.

For several years a reaction had taken place in Italy against the philosophical positivism of the liberals. There arose a disposition on the part of those in authority to turn the Italian people away from the agnostic tendencies that had been fostered and back to the recognized authority of the Catholic Church. Benito Mussolini was aware of this tendency and took full advantage of it. In all that he did, one controlling passion guided his policies—to make of his country something more than "a geographical expression" as Metternich had contemptuously called it, and something else than Lamartine's characterization as "a land of the dead." His one consuming passion was to create out of the heritage left by Dante, Da Vinci, Michelangelo, Galileo, St. Francis, Savonarola, Verdi, Garibaldi, Marconi and D'Annunzio, a country with a glorious future that should command the respect of the dominant powers of the world. He espoused the entry of Italy into the War largely because he had felt that Italy must be aroused out of a lethargy and that war would unite the Italian people. Georges Sorel, the great French Socialist, as far back as 1912, had said prophetically of Mussolini:

Our Mussolini is not an ordinary Socialist. It is my belief that some day we shall see him at the head of a mighty legion, saluting the Italian flag with his sword. He is a fifteenth century Italian, a Condottiere. He does not yet know it himself, but he

[3] (!) "My Kingdom is not of this world." L.B.-O.

is the only man of energy in Italy who can save his country from
its government's weakness.

So these two personalities, Pius XI and Benito Mussolini, so opposed in training, education and outlook, were
the predestined actors upon the stage of Italy's and perhaps of the world's future. They were to arrive at a
mutual pact, each to achieve the end most dear to his
own heart—and for motives as far removed as the antipodes.

Always in the back of Pius XI's mind, however preoccupied he was with the numerous duties of his exalted
position, there had stirred the ever-insistent Roman
Question.

Since 1870, when Pius IX went into voluntary imprisonment, it was the uncompromising contention of the
Holy See that the Supreme Pontiff of Catholicism, as
Shepherd of Souls in every land, could never be subject
to any government on earth. Because this position was
never surrendered by the Papacy, because through the
long reigns of the "prisoner popes" (Pius IX, Leo XIII,
Pius X, and Benedict XV) the monies due the Holy
See under the Law of Guarantees were never accepted
(since acceptance would imply that the Papacy was a
pensioner of the State), the torch of Papal independence
of all earthly authority was kept burning for sixty years.

As an example of an ideal that would not be surrendered, of a standard that would not be lowered, the
final victory of the principle of Papal independence by
Pius XI should shine as a classic example of the ultimate
triumph of uncompromising principle.

Many temptations arose to break the Papal resistance. The hardships entailed upon the Papacy were tremendous. The impoverishment of the Holy See, the actual poverty under which the Church continued to function, was relieved only by the contributions of the Faithful through Peter's Pence.

In order to lift the Holy See out of the morass of depleted finances, to equip her to function in a modern world, it was necessary to rescue her from this impasse, to revitalize her hierarchy, to inspire her clergy with a sense of the Church's power, to supersede the apathy and impotency that had come to seem normal, and to hearten her children everywhere and attract all eyes once more to the pole-star of religion. This Pius XI was determined to achieve when through a policy of conciliation he met the Roman problem with his customary tact, caution, prudence and courage. Already the results of the signing of the Lateran Accord have brought about within the ranks of the clergy a rededication, a resurgence of youthful energy, and a sense of pride in their Church that have been evident to those who have watched and studied the policies of Pius XI.

The old spirit of apology has given place to an aggressive virile courage to grapple with the challenge of a paganized society. Supported by Catholic Action, the clergy is prepared today to meet the terrific onslaught of material forces that have made such headway in modern society. Pius XI has created a holy pride in modern Catholics who in dark days to come will offer up their services and their lives on the altar of a reborn Faith.

Few events can be compared with the Lateran Accord in its far-reaching importance. It is more than a termination of a conflict between the Church and the State of Italy. It represents an effective official recognition of the spiritual independence of the Supreme Pontiff and of the universal character of his authority. Texts of the Treaty, the Concordat and the Financial Agreement were ready August 30, 1928. On September 3rd Cardinal Gasparri authorized Professor Pacelli (brother of the present Secretary of State) to enter into official negotiations with the Italian government. On November 22nd the King gave Mussolini full power to conduct official negotiations for the solution of the Roman Question and to sign the Treaty and the Concordat. On the 25th the Holy Father delegated Cardinal Gasparri for the same purpose. On February 7th the diplomatic representatives accredited to the Holy See were notified of the imminence of the Accord. Italian ambassadors and ministers, Apostolic nuncios and internuncios were likewise informed and were notified to apprize their governments. On February 11, 1929, the three documents which constitute the Lateran Accord were signed by Cardinal Gasparri on behalf of the Holy See and by Signor Mussolini on behalf of the King of Italy.

A few days before the actual signing of the documents a solemn *Te Deum* was sung in the Basilica of St. John Lateran to celebrate the seventh anniversary of Pope Pius XI's coronation. Large crowds flocked to the famous

old cathedral church, mother of all the churches of
Rome. It was known that Cardinal Gasparri had received
the Collar of the Annunziata and that His Holiness had
conferred upon Il Duce the Knighthood of the Order of
Christ. An air of pleased anticipation filled the streets
of Rome.

On the appointed day, in a dismal rain at about mid-
forenoon, Pacelli, Assistant Secretary of State and Legal
Advisor of the Vatican, drove up in an automobile into
the Piazza del Laterano, followed almost immediately
in a closed car by Cardinal Gasparri who had been very
ill and only recovered sufficiently to fulfill his duties as
representative of the Pope. Among the watching crowd
in the downpour outside in the piazza were several diplomats of the Curia.

The bells were striking noon when Il Duce arrived
with his Secretary and his Undersecretary of Foreign
Affairs and of Justice. The Premier proceeded up the
grand staircase into the Hall of Constantine, the ancient
council hall where Pope Leo III had been host to the
Emperor Charlemagne. Here Cardinal Gasparri greeted
Il Duce formally. For in this historic hall, so rich in
memories, the documents were to be signed. Nearby,
overlooking the table on which the papers lay was a bust
of the Pontiff, Pius XI. Very little was said by either
Mussolini or Gasparri. Both seemed impressed by the
solemnity of the hour. Cardinal Gasparri and Signor
Mussolini seated themselves at the center of the table
with the Vatican representatives at the Cardinal's right,
and the government's representatives at Il Duce's left.

After exchanging credentials and the reading of the documents by both parties, Cardinal Gasparri and Mussolini
affixed their signatures. The Pope had sent a golden pen
which he had blessed especially for the ceremony. The
very formal proceedings were relieved by a little human
touch when Cardinal Gasparri presented the pen to Il
Duce as a gift. Then formal congratulations were exchanged. The whole ceremony was very brief and simple.

The Cardinal left the council hall first, and as he
appeared on the steps in his cassock piped in scarlet and
his cape flung over his shoulder, a cheer went up from
the waiting crowd outside who had been notified of the
signing of the Accord by the salute of a gun and the
ringing of church bells. In the piazza the theological students intoned a *Te Deum* in which the Fascists joined.
Then the Black Shirts rent the air with their shouts of
Evviva il Papa, eja, eja, alalà! Acknowledging this loyal
homage to the Pope, the theological students responded
by giving the Fascists the Roman salute.

While the Accord was being signed the Pope was
addressing the Lenten Preachers in the Vatican. He
spoke to them with the intimate and affectionate words
which he can evoke so tellingly. He welcomed them at

a moment of deepest solemnity to Us personally, for it is the
vigil of the seventh anniversary of Our Coronation and the beginning of the Jubilee Year proclaimed in commemoration of
the 50th year of Our priesthood—two events which combine
to remind Us in a most awe-inspiring manner of all the graces
and mercies poured forth upon Us by God, and all our own
weaknesses and deficiencies during all these years.

For still another reason is your presence here today particularly opportune and gratifying, a reason capable in itself of lending the highest significance to this audience.

On this very day, in this very hour, perhaps at this very moment, yonder in the Lateran Palace . . . there is being signed by His Eminence, Cardinal Gasparri, Secretary of State, acting as Our Plenipotentiary, and by the Cavaliere Mussolini, acting as Plenipotentiary of His Majesty, the King of Italy, a Treaty and a Concordat. A Treaty it is that recognizes and, so far as human means can provide, secures for the Holy See, a true, proper, and real territorial Sovereignty, for hitherto no other form of sovereignty has been recognized in the world as real and proper unless it was also territorial, and which evidently belongs to him, who, being invested with the Divine mandate and the Divine representation, cannot be the subject of any earthly sovereign.

To the Treaty it has been Our will that a Concordat be conjoined, which will duly regulate religious conditions in Italy so long interfered with, subverted and devastated by a succession of sectarian governments, obedient to or allied with the enemies of the Church, even though perhaps they were not enemies themselves.

Pius tells the Lenten Preachers that he is well aware that some will be dissatisfied with the results of his labors of which not a line or phrase or word has escaped his personal study, meditation and prayer, but he adds whimsically that this is a dilemma which "even God Himself cannot escape." *Ego autem in flagella paratus sum* is the deeply-rooted habit of his life.

Pius then asks, "How can we possibly provide sure defense for the future? What of tomorrow?" To which he tranquilly replies: "We do not know. The future is in God's hands—and hence in good hands." Whatever the outcome "we shall follow the signs of God trustfully, whithersoever they may lead."

The criticisms that are bound to be levelled at the Holy See are twofold. Some will say that too little has been demanded, and some will say too much. To the former, Pius answers that he has deliberately asked the least possible amount of territory for good and weighty reasons. His deliberate desire "to act as a father toward his sons" was to render matters "not more complicated and difficult, but simpler and easier."

We would banish all alarms, by rendering unjust and unreasonable all the recriminations that will be made in the name of the superstitions of territorial integrity of the country.

[This course seems to the Holy Father] a prudent idea beneficial to all . . . one which provides for a greater tranquillity, the first and most indispensable condition of a stable peace and prosperity. For no earthly cupidity moves the Vicar of Christ. . . . He asks just enough territory to support the Sovereignty itself—just enough, as the Blessed Saint Francis said, to keep the body united to the soul. . . . We are well pleased that things are so. (Italics the author's.)

Yet, although the territory is small, considered materially— yet it is great—the greatest in the world . . . for when a territory can boast the colonnade of Bernini, the cupola of Michelangelo, the treasures of science and art contained in the libraries, in the museums and galleries of the Vatican, when a territory includes and shelters the tomb of the Prince of the Apostles, one can justly say it is the greatest and most precious in the world.

Thus, "triumphantly and tranquilly" does Pius dispose of the objections of the Intransigents.

To those who will object that the Holy See has asked too much in the economic field, the Pope replies: "If all that the Church has been despoiled of, going back to the patrimony of St. Peter, what an enormous sum it would be!" As Supreme Pontiff His Holiness cannot forget all this, for

has he not the particular duty of providing for the present and the future, for all the needs that are referred to him from all parts of the world—which, though spiritual, cannot be met without material means?

Providence does not dispense Us from the virtue of prudence [adds the Pope, again in the spirit of whimsicality] for the Catholic Church extends throughout the entire world and its needs continually increase with the gigantic development of missionary labors not to speak of the civilized countries of Europe and especially of Italy herself, where needs are numerous and grave—the needs of persons, of ecclesiastical works and institutions, deeply vital and so pitiful as to move one to tears.

A month after the signing of the Lateran Accord the Pope gave an audience to the Diplomatic Corps. The Dean, His Excellency Signor Carlo Magalhaes de Azevedo, Ambassador Extraordinary and Plenipotentiary of Brazil, addressed His Holiness on behalf of his colleagues and felicitated him on the settlement of the Roman Question in these pertinent words:

Every act of reconciliation in the international sphere merits our cordial welcome *because it is a factor and pledge of general peace.* Many scorn this idea of general peace as if it were a childish dream. We do not conceal from ourselves its many difficulties. Yet our sincere efforts must tend in that direction. . . .

During twelve centuries the Pontiff-Kings were clothed with both temporal and spiritual sovereignty. The Papacy had its nuncios and internuncios who were in full right the deans of the diplomatic corps. Thus an indestructible historic tradition testified to a visible and undeniable sign of his sovereignty. The continual presence of the diplomatic corps around the pontifical throne was maintained even during the pontificates of the four prisoner popes. Henceforth no question can arise regarding the sovereignty of the Papacy.

In response to the Dean's welcome, the Holy Father said that letters, telegrams and dispatches have been flooding the Vatican from all over the world. These messages are, said Pius, "a true plebiscite" which has been rendered not only by the nation of Italy but by the world. They are an inspiring guarantee for the future; for the tendency everywhere is for "religious pacification."

In this great and moving experience of his pontificate Pius XI's thoughts turn toward his native Lombardy and to "the dear and beautiful mountains of our youth. One has to mount high to get the loftiest point of view. One has to gain the summits—the crests. There the scenery is infinitely broader and more sublime" . . . muses the Pope of Reconciliation.

Then, like a thunderbolt in the serene sky, a speech by Mussolini in the Chamber of Deputies and another a few days later in the Senate so agitated His Holiness that he declared that he was ready to denounce the

Lateran Pact and do without the independent State of the Vatican, if Italy did not observe the letter and the spirit of the Concordat. This Papal rebuke came seventeen days after Il Duce addressed the deputies and five days after his speech in the Senate and only two days before the Papal signature was to be affixed to the Accord. Mussolini, in that spirit of crude drollery in which he occasionally indulges, declared that "We have not resuscitated the temporal power of the popes, we have buried it; we have left it just enough land to be interred in for all time." He jested about the good old times enjoyed in Rome under the rule of the popes. These remarks were resented by the Vatican as utterly uncalled for and in violation of the spirit of the Concordat. Mussolini himself later characterized them as "raw, but necessary."

It was necessary to establish with a drastic phrase what had actually occurred in the political field and to define the respective sovereignties—the Kingdom of Italy on the one hand—and the Vatican City on the other. I tried to eliminate the misunderstanding which led some to believe that the Lateran Treaty would Vaticanize Italy or Italianize the Vatican.

After Mussolini's speech on the Lateran Accord emphasizing that the Treaty would not "make the Pope a chaplain of the King, nor the King an acolyte of the Pope," only ten votes out of three hundred were negative.

But Mussolini must have felt that he had gone too far, for he ordered the police to seize the Fascist newspapers which answered the Papal denunciation.

In spite of this untoward turn of events which marred the harmony that had prevailed, the Accord was signed by the King on May 27th, and by Pius on the 30th.

In accordance with the three-fold agreement of the Lateran Accord—the Treaty, the Concordat and the Financial Agreement—the Italian government agreed to pay to the Pope seven hundred and fifty million lire in cash and a thousand million lire in five percent state bonds. The Treaty created the new Vatican City-State —a territory only slightly larger than that which the Law of Guarantees allowed—over which the Pope has absolute sovereignty. The Treaty defined the status of the residents of Vatican City and all ecclesiastical members under the Papal administration and all diplomats accredited to the Holy See. The Concordat settled questions regarding the Church's position in the Italian state and the Catholic view of marriage, and made religious instruction compulsory in secondary as well as in primary schools. Bishops were obliged to swear an oath of fealty to the Italian state.

.   .   .   .   .   .

The celebration of the signing of the Lateran Accord and the solution of the Roman Question was impressive, colorful and magnificent. Flags and banners were flung to the wind from all the palaces and public buildings, and for the first time in sixty years the Papal yellow and white fluttered in the breeze alongside the Tricolor. Though the weather continued inclement, vast crowds thronged the streets in the rain and moved about in expectant awe. The celebration of Pius' coronation was observed in a new manner—or rather in the old manner of the pre-prisoner popes. Toward the Piazza di San Pietro the motley throng of scarlet-soutaned seminarists, black-robed nuns and brown friars, black-shirted Fascists and the uniformed police and soldiers of the King mingled among the automobiles.

Within the mammoth basilica the Church dignitaries —the archbishops and bishops, patriarchs and members of the chapter of St. Peter's sat on their accustomed benches which were covered with tapestry. Everywhere were the arms of Pius XI. The Papal throne was resplendent with draperies. Velvet seats were conveniently placed so that the relatives of the Pope could watch the ceremony.

As His Holiness approached from the throne room and the procession wended its stately way slowly down the nave, a thundering shout of applause arose to greet the Pontiff-King, who, seated upon the *sedia gestatoria*, was plainly visible to all as he made the sign of the cross over the heads of fifty thousand of his children. At the penetrating fanfare of the silver trumpets the people fell on their knees at his approach like waves of the sea before the oncoming tide. At the conclusion of the Mass the Pontiff, wearing the triple tiara, once more passed through the multitudes, leaving the basilica via the Capella della Pietà to the storm of enthusiastic acclaim, as shouts of *Viva il Papa Pio Undecimo!* smote the palpitating air.

Outside, in the Piazza, the crowd of a quarter of a million quietly waited in the rain in an almost terrifying silence. Such was the intensity of their emotion that when His Holiness appeared on the loggia attended by the faithful Gasparri and his highest prelates, many fainted as the throng knelt in the pools of water to receive the Papal benediction. Fearing a demonstration, some of his Fascists asked Mussolini to disperse the crowd, but Il Duce only smiled and replied with a wry expression: "I can disperse a revolutionary mob, but I am helpless against a peaceful throng."

At nightfall, bells rang, bands played and the ancient palaces were illuminated with the old flaming Roman torches. St. Peter's was a dream as the searchlights caressed the soft mellow façade of the venerable pile.

At the Palazzo Colonna the Prince and Princess Colonna held a papal reception as in the grand old days. The Cardinal Secretary of State, Pietro Gasparri, was resplendent in his scarlet soutane while on his breast glittered a magnificent cross bestowed upon him by the Sovereign Pontiff for the services he had rendered the Holy See in liberating the Vatican. There was an air of princely grandeur singularly fitting to this mingling of the ancient house of the Colonna and the Papal dignitaries against a background of frescoed walls adorned with banners of Papal and kingly Rome. Among the guests escorted to the reception room by flaming torches were the Countess Ratti, sister of the Pope, and the Marchese Perischetti, his niece.

At the Vatican, the Holy Father was receiving a delegation of professors and students from his beloved Milan University. He seemed to have forgotten for the moment all the pomp and circumstance of his new dignity—or perhaps it became him so well that it did not appear to be new. His face lit up with quick flashes of wit and joy. He spoke as Achille Ratti of Lombardy, for in the presence of his "Ambrosians" he felt singularly at home.

So great have been the difficulties in bringing this Treaty to a successful conclusion, that I am tempted to think that a solution could be achieved only by a Pope who was also an Alpinist accustomed to tackling the most arduous ascents, and by a librarian trained to the deepest historical and documentary researches.

A free ripple of laughter echoed through the ancient hall. Where Achille Ratti was, the Milanese felt always at home.

Now that the Roman Question was settled for all time, and the nation had adjusted itself to the idea of the new status of the Pope, the Catholic public awaited the Sovereign Pontiff's first appearance in his new territory. He selected an hour of night for this public audience. The crowd, estimated at three hundred thousand, greeted their Pontiff-King with shouts of Viva il Papa-Re! as he appeared on a specially constructed sedia gestatoria carried by twelve red-robed attendants, under a red velvet canopy supported by seminary students of Rome, and carrying in his hands the Monstrance. His Holiness wore a cream-colored cloak embroidered with threads of gold. The famous flabella waved in the breeze and the constant mingling of changing colors lent a magical atmosphere of unreality to the spectacle. The cardinals in their scarlet robes with ermine capes, the

Swiss Guards, the Roman courtiers of the Papal Household in their black silk knee-breeches and ruffles—all
these moved with steady tread down the steps of the
basilica and, turning, proceeded under the colonnade of
Bernini, making the circuit of the Piazza, until they returned once more to the steps of the basilica. Then the
Pope descended from the sedia, approached the altar
erected there and, turning toward the people, he blessed
them. In the flooding searchlights, he stood revealed as
if in a nimbus of glory, while the silver fanfare resounded
in the night air. Then Pius XI, Temporal Sovereign of
Vatican State and Supreme Pontiff of the Catholic
world, withdrew to hold his first court. The crowd
watched him pass from their sight, eager not to lose the
least detail and reluctant to leave the ancient piazza that
had just witnessed a new-old ceremony, while cries of
Viva il Papa-Re! were carried beyond the colonnade of
Bernini to the outer world.

.   .   .   .   .   .

Two years after the signing of the Lateran Accord
there began a series of persecutions, street demonstrations and raids directed against Catholic Action in
Rome. These disturbances became so serious that what
had at first been hoped was an irresponsible sporadic
movement, took on the character of a centrally controlled campaign of violence. Printing presses of Catholic
Action were seized and their rooms were ransacked for
evidence to prove the Fascist-press contention that the
organization was not living up to the Papal injunction
of keeping out of politics, but was indirectly interfering

with the government. Catholic youth associations were officially banned and the organizations of students associated with Catholic Action were disbanded.

This "lightning-like police order," as Pius XI characterized the disbanding of the youth associations, created a situation so painful to His Holiness that he forbade all public religious processions, although it was the year of the seventh centenary of St. Anthony of Padua, and the anticipated celebration would, under normal conditions, have included the traditional outdoor manifestations of piety that always accompany such an outstanding occasion in the Church's calendar.

It was during the period of Papal prohibition of all religious festivities that a High Mass was celebrated in St. Peter's for Spanish religious refugees who had flocked to Rome to pour into the ear of Pius their tale of persecution at home. The author remembers that when she presented her ticket the handbags and packages of each applicant were scrupulously examined by the Swiss Guards in the atrium. It was said that a bomb had been discovered behind the altar and that every precaution had to be taken.

It was the first public appearance of the Supreme Pontiff since the publication of his famous Encyclical, *non abbiamo bisogna*, which the Boston prelate, Monsignor Francis Spellman, had smuggled out of Italy into France, in order that it might receive the circulation and publicity that the controlled press of Italy would not permit. Indeed, if it had been released in Rome, it would have been promptly confiscated. There was an air of expectancy in the faces of all of us (there were forty-five thousand within the basilica precincts) who stood awaiting the arrival of His Holiness. It seemed to the writer that the face of the Pontiff was lined with care and —from her vantage point against the red silken rope of the main aisle down which the procession passed—that Pius XI had visibly aged since she had seen him in audience two summers before. It was evident that he had been wounded in the innermost recesses of his being.

His Encyclical, on *Azione Cattolica* (*non abbiamo bisogna*) had been written and released on June 29th. It was now September. Yet the atmosphere was still tense with suppressed feeling. No document ever revealed more illuminatingly the true character of its creator than did this Encyclical, which rang out with the clarion call of righteous indignation and scathing denunciation. The accusations of the enemy were hurled back upon the assailants of the Faithful, and the indignities against the Holy See were condemned with withering irony. The swift thrust of the Pope's phrases have the shining flash of St. Michael's sword drawn from its scabbard of truth. In unmistakably clear and forceful language Pius denounced the perpetrators of the outrages directed against the Church. He held up to righteous scorn the shameful proceedings of the unruly street mobs so unwarranted and uncalled-for. He spoke bitterly of the unjust charges levelled against Catholic Action in general and Catholic youth in particular which he declared unsubstantiated by a single proof. He charged his accusers with bearing false testimony and challenged them to produce from all the documents and correspondence that they had confiscated *en masse*, a single discovery to prove their statements.

"Tell us, therefore, tell the country, tell the world what documents there are and how many of them there are that treat of politics planned and directed by Catholic Action with such peril to the State," Pius demanded. "We dare to say that no such will be found unless they are read and interpreted in accordance with preconceived and unfair ideas, which are contradicted fully by facts and by evidence and by numberless proofs and witnesses."

Wounded to the quick and in bitterness of grief and affliction of spirit, Pius does not forget to mention in an especially grateful and sensitive manner that, although the disbanding was carried out in a way and with the use of tactics which gave the impression that action was being directed "against a vast and dangerous organization of criminals," yet there were officers of the law charged with the obligation to carry out orders of suppression who "were ill at ease and showed by their expressions and courtesies that they were almost asking pardon for doing that which they had been commanded." He adds with Christ-like tenderness, "We have appreciated the delicate feelings of these officers and We have reserved for them a special blessing."

The characterization of the Church as "ungrateful" and the assertion that the priests and bishops have displayed "black ingratitude" against the party that has guaranteed religious liberty throughout all Italy, is answered by Pius with the calm response that "the clergy and the bishops and this Holy See have never failed to acknowledge everything that has been done for the advantage of religion" and that they have on many occasions expressed their genuine and sincere gratitude, rendering the charge of ingratitude insincere and untrue. In view of these substantiated facts, the abuses that ended in the recent attacks of the police "lead one seriously to doubt that the former benevolences and favors were actuated by a sincere love and zeal for religion, but rather incline to the opinion that they were due to pure calculation and with the intention of solidifying power. How can the Holy See be 'grateful'," asks Pius, "to one who, after putting out of existence anti-religious organizations . . . has permitted them to be readmitted, as all see and deplore, and has made them even more strong and dangerous inasmuch as they are now hidden and also protected by their new uniform"?

If the question of ingratitude is to be given consideration, remarks the Pope cogently, "that ingratitude used toward the Holy See by a party and by a regime that, in the opinion of the whole world, from the fact of establishing friendly relations with the Holy See . . . gained a prestige and a credit which some people in Italy and outside of it considered excessive as they deemed the favor on Our part too great and the trust and confidence which We reposed too full."

The new doctrine of stateology is castigated in the most explicit terms as "most grave in itself and destructive in its effects" when it not only consists of external action perpetrated and carried into effect but also in "principles and maxims proclaimed as fundamental and constituting a program."

The responsibility of the Church and her ministers as educational and moral and spiritual leaders does not end with the Mass and the Sacraments, the Pontiff asserts. It is contrary to true Catholic life and doctrine to believe so, and to think that all the rest of education belongs to the State. A conception which claims the youth as belonging entirely to it can never be reconciled either with Catholic doctrine or with the natural rights of the family. These false and pernicious maxims and doctrines have repeatedly been challenged and denied by the Head of the Church himself "many times during the last few years," which was the duty imposed upon him by virtue of his position. The rights of Christ and His Church and of the souls committed to her care are "inviolable rights."

Yet, the Pope continues, as Supreme Pontiff of the Universal Church he has gone out of his way to favor the compatibility of co-operation although "to others it had seemed inadvisable." He explains that he took this course in trying to find a *modus vivendi*, because he desired to believe that the actions and accusations were the exaggerated expressions of an irresponsible element "rather than, strictly speaking, part of a program." But these late occurrences have disabused the Papal mind, and consequently he must proclaim that one is not a Catholic except in name and by baptism, "who adopts and develops a program that makes his doctrines and maxims so opposed to the rights of the Church of Jesus Christ and of souls, one who misunderstands, combats and persecutes Catholic Action which, as is universally known, the Church and its Head regard as very dear and precious."

Then, in no uncertain terms, the Pope denounces the oath imposed upon the youth and the children of Italy by the new regime in which they have to swear to serve with all their strength, even to the shedding of blood, the cause of a revolution that snatches the youth from the Church and from Jesus Christ—an oath to a revolution that educates its own forces to hatred, to deeds of violence, and to irreverence. "Such an oath as it stands is illicit," concludes the Holy Father.

Then, in his deep pity for those who have to swear such an oath which is against consciences which he knows are tortured by such an obligation, since "for countless persons it is a necessary condition of their career, for bread, for life itself," he writes:

We have sought to find a way which would restore tranquillity to these consciences, reducing to the least possible the external difficulties of the situation, and it seems to us that such a means for those who have already received the membership cards would be to make for themselves before God, in their own consciences, the reservation such as "Safeguarding the laws of God and of the Church," or "In accordance with the duties of a good Christian," with the firm resolve to declare also externally such a reservation if the need of it might arise.

Not long after the publication of this famous Encyclical Il Duce's brother died; he was one of the few persons whom Mussolini really loved. Was it due to the death of Arnaldo Mussolini that the Duce sought an audience with the Holy Father? Did the Premier, in extremis, realize the slender thread that might any day snap and call him to an accounting with his Maker? In his hour of profound grief did the religion of his mother who had taught him that "Nobility of spirit is the only true nobility, it sets you apart from the common herd"—did her spirit prevail in the awful presence of death?

We know that the audience was granted and the two men who were wielding Italy's and perhaps the world's destiny, met at the Vatican in private audience for the first time. The words that passed between Il Duce and the Supreme Pontiff will never be recorded. We can only guess, from what we know of the characters and personalities of the men themselves, what their purport must have been, and from the subsequent act of Mussolini when he left the Pope's presence and knelt in prayer before the altar of the Apostle Peter in the solitude of his own meditations.

Chapter VIII

VATICAN CITY-STATE

PIUS XI will assuredly go down in history as one of the great Builder-Popes. For with the signing of the Lateran Accord there began a new phase of building in Vatican City which has proceeded energetically ever since. The cash settlement of the Italian state to the Holy See provided ample funds for the purpose. In keeping with the new needs of the times and with the added functions acquired by the restoration of temporal power, Pius XI has fitted Vatican City with every equipment that modern science has put at his disposition. The old appearance of the Vatican grounds has undergone great changes by the addition of new buildings. As one proceeds through the southern entrance at the end of the basilica, the first building to great the eye is the new Palace of Justice. Here are tried any cases of law-infringement within Vatican City. Facing the apse of St. Peter's is the Palace of the Governor which has a splendid approach. It houses all the administration offices and has fine apartments for famous visitors and an adjoining wing in which there is a private chapel for their use.

Built to receive official visitors to the Holy Father is

the handsome railway station. Its main hall of honor is lined with precious marble and on right and left are smaller halls—one for the diplomatic corps and the other for the Pontifical court. The arms of Pius XI ornament the façade and a fountain splashes within a colonnade of pillars. Next to the station is the Papal garage which shelters the motor cars (about three hundred of them) belonging to the Holy See. These cars carry the plate SCV, standing for *Stato della Città del Vaticano.*

In an old tower of the wall of Leo IV the Vatican observatory is located. Gregory XIII built a Pontifical observatory in the sixteenth century. Here was carried on the labor of making the calendar reform with which the name of this Gregory is associated. During the nineteenth century it had been used for making important meteorological and astronomical observations. After 1870 and the fall of the temporal power, the scientific work ceased and the Quirinal, which had been the home of many of the prelates connected with the Holy See, was occupied by the House of Savoy. The old Gregorian Tower became the abode of the prelates. When Leo XIII celebrated his jubilee, he was presented with some scientific instruments of rare value and he conceived the idea of restoring the observatory to its original purpose. But the old Gregorian Tower was not sufficiently commodious to house the new astronomical instruments and so Leo appropriated the old Leonine Tower which had been constructed as a defense against the Saracens in 848. A famous astronomer, Father Denza, a Barnabite, took over the work under the pa-

tronage of Leo XIII, who, on the occasion of the dedication declared that "the Church and its pastors have
never held aloof from true and solid science, either in
divine or human matters; on the contrary, they embrace
it, they favor it and contribute towards its progress with
love, so far as it is within their power." Now, under
Father Stein, of the Society of Jesus, its work is in keeping with the work of the great observatories of the world.

Next we pass on to the Grotto of Lourdes. Here Pius
XI, before his illness, came daily to pray when he went
for a stroll into the gardens.

Just beyond the Grotto to Our Lady is a building of
modest proportions which is the Vatican radio station.
It is here that the late-lamented Marconi worked inces-
santly to improve his experiments with the apparatus he
himself installed. Father Gianfranceschi, S.J. now directs
the station. It is the most powerful in the world and has
the finest equipment in existence. It has a set for radio
vision and an ultra-short wave length—the sole one of its
kind. From this station on the great days of celebration,
on feast days and on Sundays, this apparatus sends a
service and a sermon to the sick. The choir of St. Peter's
is heard from different wave lengths, and the ringing of
the bells. From this station the voice of the Supreme
Pontiff can be heard amidst the snows of the Arctic and
in the remotest reaches of the Tropics, in London and
Paris and Berlin, in New York and Chicago, in Honolulu
and the Transvaal——

The new Vatican Museum is a rose stucco building.
With the most modern method of reflected lighting

from above the great masterpieces of Giotto, Da Vinci, Raphael and others are seen at the best possible advantage. Here hangs the great Transfiguration of Raphael that draped the artist's dead body as it was carried through the streets of Rome before it found final resting place in the Pantheon. Studios for restoring works of art are located beneath the Museum where the very best and most scientific methods are employed.

Modern in every detail is the new post office. The stamps of Vatican City are much prized by collectors. The first printing brought a substantial sum into Vatican City revenue.

An *Annona*, or commissariat, has been established on the grounds of Vatican City where food and other articles can be bought by the citizens at a very reasonable price due to freedom from the state tax which prevails in Italy. There are schools for mosaic artisans and for tapestry weaving. A conservatory, containing seven hundred varieties of orchids, and several fountains, whose splashing waters are heard as one saunters through the gardens, complete the new grounds of Vatican City.

Citizenship in Vatican City is conditioned by service to the Papacy. All the inhabitants are under the jurisdiction of the Pontiff of Rome and are governed by canon law and the statute of Vatican City. They are citizens of Vatican City because they are in some degree, temporal or spiritual, attached to the service of the Pope. But not all servants and functionaries of the Pope are dwellers in Vatican City. The cardinals of the Curia live in Rome and yet are citizens of the State of Vatican City. The law on the right of citizenship and sojourn in Vatican City states that it is granted to "those who reside in a permanent manner in the City of the Vatican, for reasons of dignity, charge, office or employment, when this residence is prescribed by law, or by a regulation, or when it is authorized by the sovereign Pontiff, or in his name by the Cardinal Secretary of State—or else authorized by the Governor.

Very definite limitations are imposed upon residents in Vatican City. No vendors of any sort are permitted to ply their trade. No public meetings may be held within its walls, no one may carry arms, and no printing press may be set up nor photographs taken. No printed matter or objects of art are permitted to be sold or even given away to the public.

Since the signing of the Lateran Accord the Pope of Rome is endowed with two kinds of sovereignty—spiritual and temporal. The spiritual he exercises over all the Faithful in every part of the world—the temporal he exercises within the boundaries of Vatican City. The Pontiff has within his person full legislative, executive and judicial power.

The Governor of Vatican City is a layman who is directly responsible to the Holy Father and is selected by him because of his high moral and spiritual qualities.

When Vatican City was constituted an independent state by the Lateran Accord, it was recognized by the government of Italy that the Holy See had "full ownership and exclusive and absolute power and sovereign jurisdiction over the Vatican, as it is at present composed with all its appurtenances and dowry." A plan was appended to the Treaty indicating the limits of the territory of Vatican State, a territory comprising only forty-four hectares or 440,000 square metres (110 acres). Of these, 55,000 square metres are covered by the Vatican palace alone. Its twenty courtyards cover another 25,000. On the remaining grounds are the numerous buildings, including the accommodations for its 898 inhabitants.

Although its territory is so small and its inhabitants are so few, its importance cannot be overestimated, for the wealth of its art treasures is beyond computing, its prestige in the Catholic world is supernatural in character, and its geographical and political advantages are enormous. Rome, the cradle of ancient civilization, in the midst of the Mediterranean Sea, is in an ideal climatic zone. Rome gave its name and spiritual heritage to the civilized world, and the ancient glamour clings to the Eternal City in spite of all the changes she is constantly undergoing. No city has suffered and survived such ravages. Always she has emerged triumphant over destruction and time. Today the Eternal City seems more real and secure than any capital in the world. In comparison New York appears, to the returning American who has sojourned in Rome over a period of time, like a fantastic creation in time, which might easily fall in ruins like a stack of cards when the zeitgeist that spawned it wearies of the monstrosity. A nostalgia seizes the returning pilgrim as the steamship pulls into dock—

a spiritual nostalgia that never leaves the heart that has been under the spell of things eternal.

Vatican City contains all these eternal elements in epitome and in full flower. Though so old as to seem incredible, she yet appears eternally young! The grandeur that was Rome is here intact and flourishing. Here is a dynamo of power sending forth its potent currents to the uttermost limits of the globe. Here is a lighthouse shedding its radiance over a war-racked world. For the Papal State of today exists also as a means, an instrument, for the achievement of purposes that go far beyond the tiny limits of her periphery and the insignificant number of the population shut within her frontiers. Vatican City houses more than the eye can behold. She is more than a monument to human genius. Here the living flame of eternal verities is kept lighted and is passed on from generation to generation—from pontificate to pontificate. Whatever we have been taught, however much is true of the sins of some of her popes, there remains a lustre and an immortal glory about the Roman pontificates that defy analysis and cold logic.

No pontiff has more truly merited the title "Great" than Pius XI. He has builded not only with material things. He has made use of these agencies as instruments of spiritual power that will live on through the centuries. Pius is not great because he is brilliant in the modern sense of that much-abused word. He is great because he is wise—because he is patient and far-seeing—because he has hidden depths of spiritual reserve that are not allowed to germinate in the average man. He sees the world and he sees it whole, not through the distorted lenses of prejudice and passion, as so many of his contemporaries narrowly view it. He beholds it in the pure light of one who is above the battle, *sub specie aeternitatis.*

Yet it must not be thought that he despises any of the modern means that science has placed at the service of his age to render his labors more effective. He was quick to realize the great benefit that Marconi's invention of wireless telegraphy would put at the disposition of the Holy See as a world influence. He has had two microwave wireless stations installed in Vatican territory—one in the Vatican itself and another in his summer palace at Castel Gandolfo, twelve miles away. Marconi carried out some of his short-wave experiments between these two stations.

Pius' zeal for the promotion of science is demonstrated in his Pontifical Academy of Science of which he appointed Signor Marconi a member. This honor he conferred upon the Marchese after his first Papal broadcast from the Vatican to which many millions all over the world listened. On that occasion the writer listened in her home in Chicago and clearly heard Marconi, the great inventor of radio speak these significant words:

I speak in your most august presence, O Holy Father. The joy which this historic moment has given me is the greatest reward which I could have asked for my labors. Through my work, Your Holiness has deigned to make use of the electric waves to send across space words of Peace and Benediction to all the Faithful.

The Pope spoke in reply, thanking Marconi and his collaborators and asking God's blessing upon the installation.

Marconi was a devout man and a most illustrious example of a truly religious scientist. His life was an eloquent and emphatic affirmation to the hackneyed query: "Can a man be a scientist and a Christian at the same time?" Science signified for the genius and benefactor of mankind one of the means provided man for discovering the laws of God and of explaining these wonders to the world. Believing with all his soul that the human brain is endowed by God with the ability to make great scientific discoveries, he has proven that his own extraordinary abilities are under the will and guidance of the Creator of all wonders, and he dedicated his life to that credo.

"The more a man bends the phenomena of the universe to his will and the more he discovers," the humble genius says, "the more he will find to discover. Because of this he will realize more and more 'the infinity of the infinite.'"

Here is a robust faith that was not diminished by the "multiplicity" of the modern world into which Pius' contemporary and friend was born. It is little wonder that a scientist of so profound a mind and so reverent a spirit should be honored during his lifetime with the friendship of the ruling Pontiff of Rome—of that Achille Ratti whose soul has always responded to the beauties and scientific wonders of the universe and whose pontificate has been made glorious by his personal patronage of science and particularly by his especial solicitude for the Pontifical Academy of Science.

In a letter to *L'Illustrazione Vaticana* published in Vatican City, Marconi said after the first Papal communication over the air:

The Radio Station of Vatican City, established by His Holiness, Pius XI, carried his voice today for the first time into the mysterious realms of space.

Catholicism, which before radio, has surmounted the two barriers of distance, reforming the Universal Society by men in the truth of the Evangel, finds today, in this material instrument, a new providential means by which the August Head of the Church of Rome makes his pastoral voice heard to all the Faithful of all the earth. Swiftly and subtly as a thought, the wave of the word presses in hot pursuit the wave of the spirit, which amplifies itself with the force and the ardor of truth.

The little territorial state of the Pontiff of Rome communicated today directly with the great centers of our tormented industrial civilization, as also with the more distant and humble provinces of Christendom, where the legions of evangelical truth fight the daily and bitter struggle of the Faith.

The voice of radio which serves to invoke succor to the shipwrecked man, and which accelerates the rhythm of industrial labor for men of social affairs, is today utilized by the Navigator who has overcome the storms of history, who carries the succors of Truth and who attends to the interests of all citizens of the spirit.

The "Roman-ness" of the Church, which is evangelical catholic, reaffirms itself once more anew in the transmission of the word of the Father and the Master of Divine Truth, and who is Sovereign of that universal world of the spirit.

Radio, which amongst the conquests of science, appears to touch more intimately the realm of Immateriality, is today exalted by this service which obeys those purer and more universal interests of Catholic spirituality.[1]

This, then, is another example of the adaptability of the Church to the times. By means of the invention and perfection of radio, the Supreme Head of Catholicism can communicate directly and instantly to his flock. What a tremendous power for peace! What a potential agency for guidance in critical days ahead! That it will be dedicated to the bringing about of "the Peace of Christ in the Kingdom of Christ," no one who has followed the labors of the years of the Pontiff of Rome, Pius XI, can for a moment doubt.

. . . . . .

Papal audiences are of several kinds. There are the strictly private audiences such as those granted to the ecclesiastics, to the bishops and archbishops who, according to the requirements of canon law, are bidden to come to Rome to make their *ad limina* visits, and report concerning the condition of their dioceses. These visits are continuous, and scarcely a day passes when at least one such audience with the Supreme Pontiff is not on the agenda. It is said that Pius' knowledge of the vast, far-flung field of Catholic endeavor is so up-to-date that he constantly amazes his visitor from some remote region of the Catholic world with his extensive information and his grasp of the reality of local problems. There is also a very important daily audience with Cardinal Pacelli, the Papal Secretary of State. The Cardinal Sec-

[1] Translation by the author.

retary arrives promptly at nine o'clock bringing with him
condensed reports of news from the nuncios and internuncios, from the apostolic legates who represent the
Holy See in those countries that are in formal relation
with the Vatican. Cardinal Pacelli informs the Pope of
the very latest happenings in world affairs which he has
carefully condensed from current newspapers of the
world. Pope Pius XI's interest in press reactions to Vatican policy is never known to lag. After a survey and
discussion with the Papal Secretary of State, Pius in-
structs Cardinal Pacelli what his decisions are in regard
to the Holy See's policies, which are then sent to the
Papal representatives all over the world. These daily audiences with the Cardinal Secretary are of supreme importance to the Vatican and to the world, for it is in
these conferences that the policies of the Catholic
Church are shaped.

Then there are the lay visitors who come singly or in
groups from both the Catholic and non-Catholic world,
persons who for one reason or another desire an audience with His Holiness. Distinguished rulers or diplomats are granted private audience, as are also persons of
very humble origin who have some special information
that will illumine the Papal outlook—an exile from Spain
or Mexico, a priest who is suffering persecution in Nazi
Germany and whose parish has been singled out for its
refusal to submit to the dictum of the new state and for
continuing to give allegiance as good Catholics to the
authority of Rome. Perhaps a laywoman who has created
some new form of Catholic labor and craves Papal ap-

proval may arrange to be granted an audience to have the official seal put upon her foundation.

Hundreds of thousands of children are received yearly by the Holy Father as are also newly-married couples. It would be interesting, if figures were available, to know the number of non-Catholics who come each year to Rome, having made arrangements before leaving their own lands through some Catholic cleric in the hometown, to be received by the Supreme Pontiff of Catholicism.

It was on one of those incredible days in September when Rome is glorious with that sumptuous autumnal loveliness that seems to become her so well, that the good Maria, our devoted maid at the *pensione* off the Via Sistina, knocked at the author's door and with glowing eyes and a beaming smile announced the Papal messenger whom she ushered in with a low bow. "From His Holiness, Signora," she whispered. The young messenger drew from under his long black cape the coveted document which he held in his gloved hand as he inquired the Signora's name. Satisfied as to her identity, he handed the writer the letter, stamped with the Papal seal, that was to grant her an audience with Pius XI. It had been a wait of about two weeks since she had presented to the Secretary of the Vatican her credentials which had been carefully guarded from loss—together with her passport and American Express check-book.

On the appointed day the writer presented her document and was received with a group which seemed to be composed mostly of Italians, although there were a few who had obviously travelled from even farther than America for the privilege of an audience with His Holiness. Our Parsee friends, the Patels from Bombay, who were stopping at the same *pensione*, were in the audience hall; he in his formal full-dress, and she with her flaming sari concealed by the black robe all of us women wore, with black lace mantillas over our hair. On our left was an old Italian woman with her two sturdy grandsons whose brown eyes were big with awe and wonder as we all stood around the hall of the consistory, expectantly awaiting His Holiness' arrival. Standing opposite the great open door that revealed the staircase down which Pius was to descend, we let our eyes wander over the assembled group of about twenty-five persons who appeared to represent a cross-section of society. Several of the men looked distinguished as if they belonged to the professional class. One or two of the women's faces bore the impress of culture and refinement. For the most part, however, they were of humbler origin, people whose countenances showed they had weathered the hard storms of life.

A slight stir told us of the arrival of the major domo. He was magnificent in his traditional knee breeches and gold braid, carrying his staff which tapped lightly upon the marble floor. Then an attendant in purple and lace came toward us to inspect each one. For no breach in the rules as to dress or correct personal appearance was allowed to intrude upon the conformity which the Holy Father insists upon before he approaches each pilgrim singly to impart the individual blessing. Satisfied that all had adhered to the printed rules which had been received with the Papal letter, the major domo took up his position beside the great door to await His Holiness.

Soon we saw the figure clad in a cream-colored soutane and wearing a skull cap of the same color, descend the marble stairs and advance with the long easy stride acquired in his mountain-climbing days. Upon his breast, above the broad silk sash, rested a beautiful gold cross hung from a heavy chain. The long soutane, buttoned from neck to hem, may have added to the impression of height which we knew belied the five feet, five inches; or it may have been due to the dignified carriage; at any rate, as we knelt at the signal of the major domo's tap on the floor with his staff, Pius slowly passed before the kneeling pilgrims with the ease and keen interest of a born lover of men and with the benevolent graciousness of the Father of Souls.

Approaching nearer to where we knelt, we heard the low words of blessing spoken in mellow musical Latin, as he made the sign of the cross over each bowed head, after the symbolic Fisherman's Ring on the extended hand had been reverently kissed by each kneeling pilgrim. When Pius came to the old Italian woman, he paused to inquire whence she came and to speak a special word to each lad as he placed his hand affectionately upon first one, then the other little bent head. Tears streamed down the bronzed wrinkled cheeks as the old woman responded. It was her first visit to Rome. She had brought her grandsons to be blessed by the Holy Father. It was the supreme moment of her life, the apogee of the long years! In an ecstasy of emotion the tears fell unheeded down the furrowed cheeks. After we had received the Papal blessing and had pressed our lips upon the Fisherman's Ring, the Holy Father paused to inquire of his major domo who walked beside him if the Patels came from India, for it is said that Pius XI can place almost every pilgrim. "From Bombay, Your Holiness," answered the major domo in Italian. "From Bombay?" repeated the Pope as he smiled upon the Sun Worshippers, whose ancestors had come from Persia to India centuries ago.

That night at the *pensione*, Dr. Patel, graduate of Oxford and judge of a court in Bombay, sat with his wife in the *salotta*, reviewing the day's happening with the assembled guests. "This day's experience alone is worth the journey from Bombay to Rome," he concluded enthusiastically. "The Pope is a holy man," murmured his wife, whose cheeks reflected the glow of her flaming sari.

Chapter IX

THE STEWARDSHIP OF PIUS

IT IS difficult to sum up all the labors and achievements of Pius XI in the sixteen crowded years of his amazing pontificate. One would have to furnish a complete study of all the activities of the Catholic Church during the years since Cardinal Ratti assumed the tiara to properly appraise the full meaning and the far-reaching influence of his exceptional regime. The encyclicals, the concordats, the missionary labors, the solution of the Roman Question, his incessant work for peace, constitute a monument to the ever-growing prestige of the Holy See which non-Catholics also are glad to acknowledge and acclaim. Providence has granted to Pius XI's reign a lustre of genuine and authentic splendor rarely given to the reigns of the successors of Peter whose chair has been occupied by so many gifted men of astonishing accomplishments and of conspicuous ability. Already it is declared by many of his devoted sons that the twentieth century will go down in history as the century of Pius XI.

While it is impossible to do more than indicate in broad outline the scope and glory of his pontificate, his outstanding work for peace remains the colossal achievement that overshadows all his other labors. Not that he is the only Pope who has devoted the years of his pontificate to the cause of peace. Benedict XV, his immediate predecessor and the saintly Pius X who called Dr. Ratti to Rome, did the same; but Pius XI was privileged to dedicate himself as Supreme Pontiff of the Catholic Church to the specific task of building a permanent foundation to the edifice of peace.

All his labors in the missionary field have been inspired by the realization of the necessity, not only of converting souls to the Church, but of so conducting the work of foreign missions that an enduring peaceful collaboration among the native populations will follow as the natural consequence of removing suspicion and causes of friction among the converts. For his labors for the expansion and purification of Catholic missions, Pius XI may justly be called *The Missionary Pope*.

At the very beginning of his pontificate Pius let it be known that he was the Representative of the Prince of Peace. He analyzed the pitiable plight of the people of the world after four years of futile warfare and another four years of a false "peace" founded on greed, bred in jealousy and fostered by fear and suspicion. Hatred and the ravages of war still raged. Yet he was not dismayed, for his faith was anchored in the promise of Christ, the Prince of Peace. Undeterred by the disheartening picture which he himself drew in his first Encyclical, *ubi arcano Dei*, Pius, with undaunted courage, proclaimed that he intended to pacify and reconcile. Peace was to be his chief preoccupation. Peace would inspire all his labor.

Thus was he crowned in the solemn and majestic service of Christ the King. Thus do we acclaim him *The Apostle of Peace.*

All these holy ambitions, all his solicitudes, were directed to the fulfilment of his motto: *Pax Christi in Regno Christi.* Not a year has passed that he has not exhorted the nations to disarm. And he has made it clear that there must, first of all, be a disarmament of the heart and spirit. He has lucidly defined, as he did so masterfully in his discourse of Christmas, 1930, and in his Encyclical, *Nova Impendit,* the true conditions of Christian peace. Alas! he cries out, why do men not give ear? Why do they debase their passions? The Pontiff cries to God in accents of anguish, supplicating Him to strengthen him and support him in his work for peace. The peace of Christ cannot be realized in a civilization alien to peace. The peace of Christ can only function within the reign of Christ. For the creation and restoration of the reign of Christ he dedicates Catholic Action, and so dear to the heart of the reigning Pontiff is this organization of Catholic laymen that he declares "who touches Catholic Action touches the person of the Pope."

The return of the teaching of the Evangel can alone restore a laicized, paganized society, materialistic and sordid as ours, to peace and prosperity. He outlines the task of Catholic Action as apostolic labor guided by prayer, by word, by an able and dedicated press, by an exemplary life of charity—a life dedicated to the Divine Heart of Christ the King. The Catholic laity, with the ministry of the priests and bishops, is the true and real consecration that will bring about the Kingdom of Christ in which the peace of Christ can operate. Catholic Action, infused with Apostolic zeal, must be the ally of the Church and must attach itself unreservedly to the Church's prerogatives.

In this manner does Pius XI intend to make religion independent of every political contingency. He would leave to Caesar the things that are Caesar's, but he defends the independence and the integrity of the Church with a holy jealousy. The Church develops outside of and independent of parties and its sole task is to penetrate the Christian spirit into the men and social institutions in the midst of which Providence has placed it. Such is Catholic Action, the soul and spirit of the pontificate of Pius XI. Quite accurately might Pius XI be proclaimed the *Pope of Catholic Action.*

Ending the long struggle between the Church and the State, the Lateran Accord signed by Pius XI bridged for all time the former antagonism, for the Pope agreed to remain outside of international politics—*except when invited to participate;* but the Papacy by no means relinquished its right and duty to moral and spiritual leadership in the world. Indeed, by placing herself above parties and states, the Church has legalized a spiritual supremacy that leaves her free to fulfil her mission of peacemaker and to condemn unChristian acts impartially and courageously. For instance in his message to the cardinals on Christmas Day, 1930, the Pope declared: "Peace is made difficult because the spirit of peace does not possess the intelligence and hearts of men, because of an unequal distribution of privileges and burdens, of rights and duties, of participation in the fruits which can only be produced by their friendly co-operation, *because there reigns a hard, egotistical nationalism*, which is the same as saying hatred and envy—ambition for hegemony and mastery in the place of respect for all rights, even those of the weak and small." (Italics the author's.)

But whether Pius XI will be remembered in history as the Pope of the Missions, the Pope of Reconciliation, the Pope of Catholic Action, we are confident that he will always be spoken of as *the Pope of Peace*, in company with the sainted Pius X and the "War-time Pope," Benedict XV, whose *via dolorosa* was trodden through those disheartening years of ceaseless effort to bring a mad world back to sanity. For whether Pius XI has bent his noble mind to the more efficient achievement of missionary labor, or to the nurturing of the faithful seed of Catholic Action, or to the successful solution of the Roman Question, or to the writing and sending forth of his famous encyclicals to the ends of the earth—in all that he has promoted and achieved, the underlying urge, like the *motif* of a great composer that recurs again and again in the masterpiece, lest in the intricacies of the vast composition the thread and source of inspiration be lost, has been reiterated and restated, reaffirmed and reinforced time and again, to strengthen and support, to succor and sustain, to plead and protest in a crescendo of affecting accents the theme of his pontificate—peace, peace, peace!

. . . .

Those individuals privileged with frequent access to His Holiness, Pius XI, like the cardinals and high ecclesiastics in Vatican circles and more particularly Cardinal Pacelli (who upon Cardinal Gasparri's retirement to private life, succeeded that great prelate as Papal Secretary of State), may be said, perhaps, to know at first hand the innermost workings of the Papal mind. The sole source of such knowledge for the less favored is through the medium of his writings as revealed in his encyclicals.

All the pastoral letters of Pius XI reveal the careful mind of a trained scholar, the humility of a truly great soul, the undaunted courage that can essay spiritual mountains and scale insuperable difficulties with clear-sighted prudence and disciplined patience. In spite of the numerous duties and interruptions that must have accompanied the writing of these letters, one feels there is nothing hurried, no thought carelessly expressed, no decision hastily arrived at. The abiding faith that shines through these documents is not the result of a detached mind dwelling in an ivory tower, but rather it is the habitual attitude of an experienced captain who does not minimize the perils of the storm, but whose steady hand on the helm and calm gaze facing the troubled sea, are fortified by a confident awareness that a Supernatural Pilot stands behind him—a Pilot who can not only safely steer the ship through every danger, but can calm the angry sea as well.

One is struck by the simplicity of the encyclicals of Pius, so that he who runs may read; by the felicity of the style; their easy flow even in translation. They seem to bear witness to Pius' admiration for the letters of St. Francis de Sales, "whose writings are easy to understand and can be read with great pleasure" and whom he nominated "the Heavenly Patron of all Writers." We feel His Holiness' advice to writers "to express their thoughts clearly and in beautiful language so that readers will the more readily come to love the truth," has been the guiding inspiration of his own messages. They reveal a character in which "the union of strength and meekness" which he stresses as the peculiar grace of St. Francis de Sales, is an active principle.

Three great encyclicals: *On the Education of Youth, On Christian Marriage* and *On the Reconstruction of the Social Order* give the reader a comprehensive idea of the mentality of the Holy Father. They compass the major problems of modern society which, unless solved, will destroy all that Christian civilization has built up through the travail of two thousand years. Unless the family unit is preserved, the western world will disintegrate and perish. Unless youth is educated to the full meaning of responsibility through a careful training, not only of the mind, but even more of the heart and will, the future of human culture presents a dubious outlook; and unless there is created a spirit of civic concern, an unselfish devotion to the larger good of the community, of the state and of the society of nations, through a constructive program based on morality and religion, wars between the classes and the nations will surely wreck the accumulated wealth and treasures of the ages.

Because the Catholic Church has throughout her history looked at the world, and has contributed so magnificently to the flowering of civilization, through an approach *sub specie aeternitatis*, it is urgent and fitting that the voice from the Vatican, speaking with the authority of the exalted responsibility it assumes, should be listened to and pondered over with all the seriousness the troubled times demand. The fleeting panaceas of well-meaning hasty reformers do not suffice to meet these grave issues that baffle the stoutest heart. A steadier influence, a firmer authority, a wiser counsel, must prevail if the chaos that threatens to overwhelm the world is to be brought to ordered sanity.

Pius XI, in unmistaking phraseology, has invited all faiths to participate with him to defend the Church's institutions. He begs that all differences be submerged so that the world's forces may work together toward the achievement of that longed-for peace which is the crying need of our day.

Implicit in Pius' gospel of peace, and conditioned by it, is his gospel of Social Justice which found eloquent expression in his Encyclical, *Quadragesimo Anno* (In the Fortieth Year) given to the world on the occasion of the fortieth anniversary of Leo XIII's great message, *Rerum Novarum, (On the Condition of the Working Classes)*. In this document Pius XI amplifies and brings up to date the teachings of Leo. Together, the two Encyclicals form a consistent body of social doctrine, declared by many able statesmen to be the only guide and answer to the blatant injustices in the industrial and economic disorders of our time. The whole problem of capital and labor, of class strife, and of the international money power which hold in their hands "the very soul of production since they supply its life-blood, so that no one dares breathe against their will," is examined with the courageous impartiality demanded by these basic aspects of the modern chaos we have inherited.

If, in time, the world will listen to "the better way" advocated by these two great Pontiffs, society may yet be saved from the suicidal class warfare advocated by the followers of Karl Marx and exemplified in modern Russia, cultivated in France and in "loyalist" Spain under cover of the "United Front." Fifty years ago Leo XIII foresaw and warned the world what would happen if the discontented and underprivileged classes followed the siren voice from the British Museum.

At the inauguration of the World Catholic Press Exposition in the spring of 1936, which was represented by journalists of forty-five nations of Europe and America and by fifty-three regions of Asia, Africa and Oceanica, after deploring the absence of "two great countries and two great peoples" (Russia and Germany), Pius XI warned those present of the perils that beset our modern times, perils not only to the cause of religion but to the very fabric of the entire social order.

The Pontiff gave a message to take back to the communities whence the delegates came. In unequivocal words that permit of no misunderstanding or misinterpretation he bade those present convey his avowed purpose of "providing remedies and means of defense against neo-paganism, to which immorality allies itself easily and almost inevitably, even under the varnish of a civilization materially refined. . . ."

"You will say, dearest sons. . . . what the Vicar of Christ does not fear to say aloud, and that not only as Common Father of all the Faithful, but also and *above all as a man of his day*, not only for the good of the Church of which He is the Head, but also for the general good, that the Catholic Church is the only and irreplaceable preserver of true and authentic Christianity." For, asks the Pontiff pertinently, "What remains . . . outside the Church, after the devastation caused by so-called free thought, by liberalism and pretended reformations? . . . And in the Catholic Church we possess, at this moment, the providential aid of Catholic Action, which was also the efficacious collaborator of the first Apostolic Hierarchy in the evangelization of a world under the yoke of ancient paganism."

"We have intentionally said that We are speaking not only as Head of the Catholic Church, but also and above all as a man of our day . . . as a witness and participant in the events which menace our contemporaries and the institutions which frame and develop their daily individual, family and social life. We speak thus . . . because from the point of view of recent definite happenings, *We are more painfully preoccupied with the purely human and worldly social and government institutions than with the Catholic Church herself.* . . . For the Church is a Divine Institution, favored with Divine promises. The forces against Her may become more

threatening, their assaults more and more violent or insidious, but it remains written: *non praevalebunt.*"
(Italics the author's.)

It is a mistake for governments to put obstacles in the path of the action of the Church, for by so doing they are denying themselves the invaluable contribution that the Church alone can give to public security, to social well-being, and to true peace.

In conclusion the aged Pontiff declared the Exhibition of the World Catholic Press "a true symbol, a real example, an efficacious instrument, a fervent and hopeful invocation, that in many languages says to all nations . . . peace, peace, peace."

To the frightful cry, *Sans Dieu,* the Exhibition replies with the confident, affectionate, liturgical prayer *Mane nobiscum, Domine* . . . Abide with us, Lord: a cloudy twilight, which seems to herald a still darker night, hangs over the whole world: Abide with us and . . . let your light shine in the darkness and guide us: Abide with us. *Mane nobiscum, Domine.*"

.   .   .   .   .   .

Clear-spoken and frank in his denunciation of evil, however highly placed, Pius displays an untiring and uncompromising will in combating the perverse spirit which animates the leaders of the people who stir up strife among the nations and classes. But he does not let the matter rest there. In a spirit of compassion and fatherly solicitude he points out a better way, a way practical and feasible, a way tested by two thousand years of experience of the Christian Church.

The indomitable will displayed by Pius during the days and nights of racking pain when his physician gave no hope to a waiting world and his death seemed imminent, was so sublime as to call forth expressions of astonished admiration from many American non-Catholic sources. An editorial, dated January 26, 1937, in the *Chicago Daily News*, rose to the high occasion declaring that Pope Pius XI "shows forth in fullest measure the serene elevation of the spirit over the flesh . . . Unmindful of himself, he almost hourly exercises a dauntless and devotional solicitude for the cause of the Church and for peace among mankind. To such a soul there can be no reality in dissolution." Vatican circles declared that his mind seemed more lucid, if anything, than usual; and his memory clearer than ever. To those nearest to him, in reply to anxious queries about his condition, he replied in a Latin phrase, paraphrasing St. Martin: *Ne recuso dolorem, peto laborem.* It was enforced idleness, not pain, that irked him. The fear that he might be incapacitated for a long time and unable to resume his duties as Supreme Pontiff; the memory of his brother Fermo's protracted illness caused him profound concern for the welfare of the Church. Accordingly, through the weeks of intense suffering, he seemed determined to ignore his own condition as much as possible; to carry on all his duties as Head of the Church, and to pursue a normal routine as far as his physical torments permitted. Cardinal Pacelli was in almost constant attendance at his bedside, receiving advice and instructions on weighty Church matters. His Holiness sent

a radio message to "pray for the re-establishing of peace
in a world that needs it badly." He sent a message of
sympathy for the flood victims in the United States,
granted audiences to numerous ecclesiastics, and by
every means kept in touch with Church and world affairs.
During his long illness from the time he was stricken
on December 5, 1936, until, unassisted, he celebrated
his first Mass at the altar of his private chapel, March
19, 1937, although on the threshold of his eightieth
year, the Pope's demeanor was an unparalleled example
of a rigorously disciplined mind, an unconquerable will,
and a sublime spirit.

As late as November 15, 1937, Cardinal Mundelein,
in a letter to the clergy and Faithful of his own diocese,
holds up the example of the Pope, Pius XI, as "a model
and exemplar of every Christian Bishop, priest and layman," declaring that "at death's door, he stood forth
as a heroic figure and an example and consolation to all
of us of every race and creed."

During this trying period the long-awaited Encyclical,
Divini Redemptoris, condemning atheistical Communism, made its appearance. In this new message Pius
urged that "all differences be submerged so that the
world's forces of all faiths may be arrayed to defend its
institutions." He denounced Communism as "a system
full of errors . . . in opposition both to reason and divine revelation . . . subversive to social order," resulting in the destruction of the very foundations of society.
Not minimizing in the least the very real abuses of the
economic order, Pius urges the employers of labor to

stand behind the Church to see that Justice is done; for, deceived by rash promises, the people are following false prophets. In the front line of battle against Communism should stand the priests supported by religious groups of laymen. Let those who, blinded to the real nature and inevitable results of the victory of such false propaganda, who let themselves be deceived into lending their aid toward the triumph of a doctrine intrinsically wrong— let all such know that they will fall the first victims of their error, warns the voice of Pius XI.

For the destruction of such pernicious doctrines and practices the Pope invokes the collaboration of all believers, renewing his invitation extended to them five years previously in *Caritate Christi* that "all those who do not want anarchy and terrorism ought to take energetic steps to prevent the enemies of religion from attaining the goal they so brazenly proclaim to the world." For, continues His Holiness, "the Church undertakes the mission confided to her by Christ, of constructing a Christian society" and resists unto victory all attacks against her. This is her duty and her responsibility, for "this anti-God campaign shakes society to its very foundations."

In a second Encyclical in the same week, Pius sent a message to the German Catholics, which, like the Letter, *non abbiamo bisogna*, was placed in the hands of trusted emissaries and smuggled by airplane through the press censorship—this time into Germany—and there read in the pulpit of the Berlin Cathedral by Bishop von Preysing. In this Papal document the Holy Father charges the Nazi government has broken the Concordat of 1933 and has rendered it "intrinsically valueless."

If its terms were not kept that is not the fault of the Church; the other side made unfair interpretations of the Concordat, evaded its provisions, undermined its content, and finally more or less openly violated its stipulations and the unwritten law governing its actions.

Pius says he signed this document "despite grave misgivings" because he believed it to be "to the interest of the Church and the German people." The rebuke to the assertion that Nazism is *Gottgläubig* is answered by the scathing words:

He is not *Gottgläubig* who merely knows how to use that word oratorically. Whoever raises the concepts of race, or people, for the state, or the form of government beyond mundane evaluations and makes heathenistic ideals of them, falsifies the divine order of things.

In conclusion the Encyclical ends with these solemn words:

God is our witness that we have no more earnest wish than the reestablishment of real peace between the State and the Church in Germany. If, however, through no fault of ours, peace is not to come, then the Church of God will defend its rights and liberties in the name of the All Highest, whose arm, even today, has not been shortened.

To the German Catholics Pius promised:

We shall not fail to continue to champion your rights before the leaders of your people, irrespective of temporary success or failure, and obedient only to our conscience and our duties as Shepherd, we shall continue to oppose an attitude that seeks to stifle guaranteed rights by open or covert show of force.

To those Nazis who charged "unfairness" against the method of smuggling the Papal letter by airplane into Germany, it should be remembered that the Holy Father employed this step only as a last resort. Various Vatican notes to Germany had remained unanswered and the government had refused to receive Catholic bishops for a conference on Church matters.

A third Encyclical to Mexican Catholics appeared within a few days. This was an Easter eve letter, appealing to Mexico's clergy and laity for a "greater intensification of the Christian life" in order that they might have "true peace and prosperity." There was no rebuke in this pastoral letter which gave high praise to the American bishops who assisted the Mexican hierarchy by erecting a seminary for Mexican students in the United States. Pius urged the Mexican laity to co-operate with the clergy "in the intensification of the Christian life in good works in every field of activity, private and public, assisting the needy classes religiously, morally and economically with social Christian good works."

Then Easter morning came. The great basilica of St. Peter's was jammed with the Faithful from all lands, and thousands waited outside in the Piazza for the first appearance of His Holiness since that day in early December when he was stricken. Almost four months of anxious suspense were rewarded by the participation of the Holy Father in the Mass at the altar. At the end of

the Mass the Pontiff read aloud the *Benedictus*. Then
he was borne out on the *sedia*. The pent-up enthusiasm
of the crowd once more broke loose. Among the shouts
of the Italians' *Viva il Papa!* could be heard by those
standing near, a strong German *Heil!* from a group
standing at attention giving the Nazi salute. The Pope
was then carried up to the balcony of St. Peter's by a
specially constructed elevator. There, standing below in
the raw March wind, a quarter of a million of the Faithful shouted and cheered and wept. Tears streamed down
the cheeks of the people as they knelt in thanksgiving
that their Shepherd had been granted his prayer and had
lived to witness and participate in the Easter celebration.

Rome has witnessed many majestic triumphs. No city
can equal her in the glamour and splendor of her pomp.
But this spectacle was different from the triumph of a
Caesar returning from his martial victories. The pagean-
try was there, but beneath the formal ceremony there
was a heartfelt enthusiasm, unpoisoned by dark con-
spiracies or sinister rumblings of discontent. What a
lesson for temporal rulers, for dictators and political
heads of states! What a triumphant manifestation of the
spirit over the flesh! What a victory of love over hate
and strife!

· · · · · ·

As early as possible after his partial recovery, Pius was
eager to leave the Vatican and Rome for the higher land
of Castel Gandolfo, the summer residence built by
Urban VIII in 1629 and since completely renovated and
modernized by himself, where he might breathe the

clearer air and find much-needed relaxation on his model farm with its pedigreed fowl and livestock. In the cool of the evenings, gazing over at the Alban hills, he could sit and dream of the foothills of his native Desio and of those loftier heights of the spirit whence cometh help.

There was a slowing down of duties, though no cessation of them during the summer of 1937. Audiences for married couples and for other pilgrims were given. Cardinal Pacelli came to keep the Pontiff informed on world events. In the autumn Pius seemed to wish to tarry as long as possible, but on his return from Castel Gandolfo in late November he stopped the car in which he was driving back to the Vatican so that he might inspect the new approach to St. Peter's from the Tiber, an approach created by the demolition of old houses and named the Via della Conciliazione to commemorate the Lateran Accord.

One of his first public acts upon his resumption of duty was the inauguration of the pontifical Roman Atheneum, built out of his own private purse, at St. John Lateran. It was noted that although precautions were taken to spare him needless exertion at the ceremonies at which he presided and gave a twenty-minute address, his color was healthy and his gestures vigorous and decided.

On December 13th he bestowed the Red Hat on five new Cardinals, one of whom was his former secretary, Pellegrinetti, whom we remember at Warsaw, and who had been serving as Papal Nuncio in Jugo-Slavia. Pius used the occasion to deplore publicly the Far Eastern conflict and inveighed against "men responsible for the destinies of nations," who "despise the sacred duties of religion and push their temerity so far as to rebel against the Divine Majesty itself."

Among the motives the Pontiff enumerated for his own special gratefulness, Pius cited the divine assistance received during his illness and the joy he felt over the recent Eucharistic congresses in which he was present through his legates, experiencing the pious and public testimony of devotion to a common Father and the faith and concord of the Catholic community.

Chapter X

PEACE AND THE PAPACY

FROM the outset of his reign Pius XI began the task of reorganizing the Church for the fulfilling of her mission in a modern world. Rome, as we have said before, is the world's most sensitive barometer, the best equipped spiritual observatory on earth. Here, on Vatican Hill, Pius saw the trends of the times. He witnessed the disaffected elements, betrayed by a "war to end war" and a shameful "peace," increasing and spreading their doctrines of class warfare. That *triangolo doloroso*—Mexico, Russia, Spain—afflicted his soul, for here he saw the doctrines of Karl Marx bearing their logical harvest of thistles, tares and brambles. The Church denounced these new saviors of society who hoped to bring about a new order by destroying the fruits of Christian culture painstakingly planted over a period of twenty centuries. Through an international network of propaganda they were seeking to destroy the Christian Church, that great agency of organized religion without which we cannot conceive of European civilization. In the name of humanity they were shooting or starving millions of human beings.

But Pius saw also the yearning of the peoples, of those

inarticulate masses of the common folk to whom Leo
had turned, for the human right to live peaceably, to
sow, to reap, to love and propagate their kind in security
and decency; and with unerring insight he began to prepare the Church to answer this awakening desire, to
guide it back to the Catholic ideal of Unity, Authority,
Peace. In this labor and dedication he signed thirteen
new concordats. Even the staid *Encyclopaedia Britannica*, which surely cannot be charged with prejudice
in favor of Catholicism, declares that "it is now apparent
that the world has, in Pius XI, a great force making for
righteousness—a new factor has entered into the relations of the nations." [1]

After the settlement of the Roman Question Pius
knew that there still remained the world-wide state of
revolt which he characterized as the lineal descendant of
the moral anarchy brought about by the nationalistic
aspirations of European powers and aggravated by the
sectarian spirit of Protestantism. The ideal of a united
Christendom which was so closely approximated in the
thirteenth century, had been superseded by the ambitions of the princes of Europe and their inevitable
series of dynastic wars. The War of the Spanish Succession in the seventeenth and eighteenth centuries split
Europe into fragments. Pius II (1458-1464) had foreseen the logical consequences, and called the Princes of
Europe to Ancona. Their refusal to heed his call spelled
the end of Papal leadership and resulted in the further
dismemberment of the continent into the sorry picture

[1] Fourteenth Edition.

of the checkered map the Versailles Treaty completed. The Protestant Reformation exaggerated the denial of all authority when it proclaimed the individual judgment supreme. The splitting up of Protestantism into numerous petty sects has been the scandal of Christendom. The complete lack of moral authority which exists today gives grave concern no less to serious-minded Protestants than to Catholics themselves—although they may not trace its pedigree with the same uncompromising logic.

Religion, instead of being a unifying principle among mankind, became a disruptive force in society, and disputes and nationalistic rivalries have continued ever since, culminating in the Great War and overshadowing our contemporary world with ominous clouds of black despair. The cleavage between the spiritual and the material life has become more and more marked. The decay of religion was the inevitable result of the denial of a central spiritual authority. The guidance of the Church had given way to skepticism, to an exaggerated intellectuality, to a one-sided education of the mind—to the neglect of the character and the spirit of man. Revolution was in the air and a mad kind of intoxication that rationalized itself in slogans such as *Liberté, Egalité, Fraternité*. Concepts began to be lost in a new jargon of meaningless phrases. Such was the world need as Pius XI saw it.

.   .   .   .

At Monza where Achille Ratti attended school for two years at San Pietro Martire's, there is a Duomo which he must have often entered to pray. His eager

young eyes must have been fascinated by a treasure
there, enclosed in a glass case like a monstrance, in
which is enshrined the iron crown of his Lombardy. He
doubtless knew its history, how Gregory the Great bestowed it upon Theodalinda, the beautiful queen of the
Lombards, how it had rested upon the mighty head of
Charlemagne, how Frederick Barbarossa wore it and
Charles V, how the great Napoleon crowned himself
Emperor with it. Precious and holy the relic is, because
within the iron crown is an inner crown of iron, beaten,
it is said, out of one of the nails of the cross. Did Pius
XI's thoughts, which we know reverted to his native
home on the plains of Lombardy when the shouts of
Viva Pio, il Papa-Re! arose from the throats of hundreds
of thousands in the great Piazza di San Pietro, dwell
upon the ancient iron crown in the Duomo of Monza?
If, by placing this emblem on the head of a future ruler
of a united Europe, peace might ensue once more and
art might flourish and men might be permitted to live
free from the hell of war, then may the vision of another
pope placing the crown on another Charlemagne live
again for the pacification and sanity of the world!

However quixotic the vision of a reunited Europe may
seem, it is surely the acme of sanity to work for a modus
vivendi among the nations of the world. To do this some
authority must be recognized as conclusive. The League
is dead. The seizure of Manchuria by Japan gave it its
first fatal stroke. The reoccupation of the Ruhr by Germany dealt it the second blow which reduced it to the
pitiable state of incurable invalidism. The Ethiopian

adventure by Italy finished the League. Its death throes were heard in all the chancelleries of the world. Its burial is long overdue. Some impartial arbitrator with clean hands must be invoked, whose decisions will not be suspect, whose interests are universal, and whose deliberations can be trusted to be carried on in the spirit of fairness, because they are founded on justice and humanity.

The glamour has been stripped from war. Victors and vanquished alike pay the hideous toll of modern warfare, which strikes down the defenseless, the aged, the little ones, with ruthless fiendishness. There are no longer any rules in the devil's game. International law has become a mockery. Innocent non-combatants are crushed beneath the juggernaut with pitiless unconcern. The harvest of corpses, after an air raid, are thrown into a cart for common burial like carcasses of cattle from the stock yards. In Shanghai such unspeakable scenes were enacted only yesterday and the science of motion-picture photography brought the sickening story to the news reels of New York and Chicago. They tell the tale of the cheapness of human life in this boasted year of our Lord, 1937! Callous beyond description are these scenes of carnage.[2]

All the amenities of international intercourse are suspended in modern warfare. The loss to humanity in man-power, in disease, in maimed public charges, in poverty and economic chaos, in depression and revolution, is in-

[2] Profiteering permitted by the United States government in scrap iron to Japan places a goodly share of responsibility upon our own shoulders.

calculable. All that two thousand years of Christian civilization has built up in the joyous expression of creative power, in blood and tears, in courage and laughter, in heroic effort and patient travail of spirit, is threatened with destruction unless the war-god is chained.

Who in all the world is better fitted to grapple in a just and impartial manner with the international tangle than the Pope? There must be an arbiter—some authority whose moral position cannot be gainsaid, whose motives are not under suspicion, whose love and compassion reach out to all mankind as to a common family—someone in whom there is confidence that a just judgment will be a foregone conclusion. *There must be a Truce of God.* Who is so well qualified as the Pope to exercise moral suasion in place of a resort to force? This does not mean that the world must become universally Catholic. Pius XI has invited all men of good will to join him in a crusade against anarchy and war, and he would be the first to welcome a *modus vivendi* and a *modus operandi* for the accomplishment of so worthy and necessary a collaboration for the achievement of peace on earth.

Nationalism, in its logical apotheosis of the totalitarian state, is the root of the evil threat of war and of all wars—whether declared or actual. It arose in its extreme expression because the Have-Nations have been unwilling to relinquish their hold on their ill-gotten gains, and the Have-Not-Nations—Japan, Italy and Germany—(for the self-preservation of their citizens whom they must feed and to assuage their humiliation) have resorted to force to take what has been withheld from them by greed.

Class warfare is the second enemy of peace. Humanity must rise or fall together. One class cannot annihilate another. Individuals can be "liquidated," but classes have a way of persisting—or exchanging places. A classless society cannot even be approximated except through the practice of Christian principles and Christian brotherhood.

The Papacy, possessing neither army nor navy nor territorial ambitions, wanting nothing for itself other than the salvation of men and of society, is the one organized force that exists in the world today under a moral and spiritual compulsion, ably equipped as an ideal agency to act for the promotion of international collaboration. Because it is freed from selfish national interests that clash and fight for advantage, because it has accepted the dual rôle of Church and State in society, because with the signing of the Lateran Accord the long conflict is at an end and the Church's function is clearly defined, the Papacy is free to exercise its influence in its true and proper mission of religious and moral leadership. This leadership is imperative, not only for the survival of Christianity itself, but also for the peace of the world, and for the preservation of western civilization.

. . . . . .

The idea of invoking a Truce of God to call a halt to the destruction that flares up today in the civil war of Spain and in the streets of Shanghai, and tomorrow in

some other theatre where the flames of hatred and in-
justice threaten a terrorized populace, is not new nor
fantastic. In the Middle Ages such a truce was invoked.
It dated from the eleventh century and arose amid the
anarchy of feudalism as a bulwark to supersede the help-
lessness of the civil authorities and to enforce respect for
the public peace. There was prevalent all over Europe an
epidemic of petty private wars which converted the continent into an armed camp of bristling fortresses. Indeed
every man's castle was a fortress and the countrysides
were overrun with armed bandits who held nothing
sacred and whose depredations extended even to the
sanctuaries of religion.

At first the Truce of God was very restricted in its
scope but later it was enlarged to embrace ever wider
areas. The Council of Elne in 1027 forced a truce from
Saturday night until Monday morning—thus sanctifying
and rendering inviolable the Sabbath. This modest beginning was the germ of the Truce of God. The prohibition was later extended to apply to all the holy days
consecrated to the Mysteries of Christianity. A further
extension included Advent and the forty days of Lent.
Thus the scourge of war was at least limited in its potential destructive force. This curtailment of the ruthless
power of armed conflicts to create anarchy and the determination to insure some immunity from the hazards
of warfare was enforced by the Church's powerful
weapon of excommunication.

The Truce of God spread from France to Italy and
Germany and the ecumenical council of 1179 still fur-

ther extended the scope of its influence to the whole Church.[3] In this manner the problem of the public peace which was the goal and craving of the Church in the Middle Ages was given the force of an authority that was acceptable to all.[4] Such was the vast influence of the authority of the Holy See that the Landfrieden and the communes followed the impetus given by the Church until war was finally restricted to international conflicts.[5]

The idea of the Pope acting as mediator is also not new nor untried. Even Bismarck, as late as 1885, after the failure of the Kulturkampf, gave concrete expression to his new policy of co-operation with the Church by recognizing where impartial and just decisions might be expected to reside when he called upon Leo XIII to settle the dispute between Germany and Spain over the Caroline Islands. This dispute was amicably settled to the mutual satisfaction of both countries until Germany finally paid a handsome price for the Islands which she had developed with her own capital.

In his book, *The Papacy and World Affairs*, Dr. Carl Conrad Eckhardt, Professor of History of the University of Chicago, cites two modern Americans to whom the idea of Papal arbitration has appealed. Mr. Victor J. Dowling, former presiding Justice of the appellate division of the Supreme Court of New York, in a baccalaureate address in June, '31, declared: "What the world needs today is respect for some central authority which

[3] Canon XXI *De treugis servandis*, a part of Canon Law of Gregory IX, *De Treuga et pace*.

[4] *La paix et la treve du Dieu*, Semichon, Paris, 1859.

[5] *Gottes und Landfreiden*, Huberti, Ausbach, 1892.

would be free from suspicion. The Pope might be the Arbitrator between nations." The Rev. John M. Phillips of Hartford, Conecticut, made a statement even more startling when he said that "all Christians and Jews should appeal to Pope Pius XI to lead a world movement against war, to end war through a religious truce similar to those of mediaeval times."

Beginning with the reign of Leo XIII and continuing through the pontificates of Pius X, Benedict XV and up through the sixteen years of Pius XI's astonishing activity, the Catholic Church has entered upon a renaissance whose full fruition is not yet consummated. The Holy See is the sole remaining hope for bringing peace and tranquillity to a distracted world where the diplomat's futile, half-hearted measures leave the real causes of war untouched as they flutter about in an aimless endeavor to delay the deluge that threatens.

When Czar Nicholas II invited Leo XIII to send a representative to the Hague Conference in 1889, along with invitations sent to all the governments of the world, the good intention was frustrated and rendered still-born by the Italian government through its minister of foreign affairs, Admiral Canevero. Queen Wilhelmina, who was to act as hostess to the conference, and the Czar were jointly notified that the participation of the Holy See in the forthcoming negotiations would be regarded as an affront to the Italian government since it would seem to imply an acknowledgment of the temporal authority of the Papacy. Hence the omission of an invitation to the Holy See by the Dutch government.

It was then that the true stature of Leo was brought into relief against the suspicious background of the other powers. Far from making a public protest at the slight, Leo blessed the deliberations of the conference, commending the spirit of the peace negotiations and taking the congress under his protection. His letter to the bishops was published far and wide. Not a hint of injury at the affront offered his person and the Holy See! In a letter to the Queen of Holland the great Leo thanked her for her good intention of inviting him to send his representative and he expressed the hope that the conference would achieve its desired aim of establishing peace in the world. He promised that, as Head of the Church, he would do all within the limited power permitted him to promote the true cause of peace. The Papal calm and dignity was an example of spiritual elevation that all the world recognized. It was in radiant contrast to the spirit animating the congress whose actions seemed motivated more by preventing the Pope from being treated as an equal sovereign than by a genuine desire for peace. Yet at the second Hague conference in 1907 no invitation was extended to the Holy See.

We have seen how the heart of Pius X was broken by the war and how he refused to bless the Austrian army. On his death-bed he is said to have moaned: "We should have stopped the War—we did what we could."

It was left for Benedict XV, who proclaimed himself "the Shepherd of souls in both camps" to make repeated appeals to the powers to seek peace. In 1914 and in 1915 when these appeals were sent to the warring governments, only the Central Powers answered the Papal communications that called upon the leaders to end the "senseless slaughter" and to proclaim a truce of God. The Allied powers ignored Benedict's notes and President Wilson's answer was so framed as to render all mediation by the Pope impossible. Wilson was said to have resented the Papal interference. Yet his famous Fourteen Points suggest that they were modelled on Benedict's seven-point program of peace. On his death-bed Benedict affirmed: "We willingly offer our life for the peace of the world." These words encompass the motif of his pontificate for the cause of religious pacification.

Since the release of the secret treaties we know why France, Great Britain and Italy paid no heed to the notes of Benedict. France, Great Britain and Russia had promised to support such opposition as Italy should make to any proposal in the direction of introducing a representative of the Holy See in the peace negotiations.

In view of the repeated refusals of the European states to permit Papal participation in the peace negotiations at the Hague or to consider the good offices of Benedict XV when, as early as 1914, he called a truce on Christmas Day and repeatedly sent pleading letters to the heads of the governments of the contending forces during the prolongation of the Great War, it is small wonder that when Pius XI signed the Lateran Accord he agreed not to interfere in international politics except when invited and unless the contending parties to a dispute appeal to the Holy See's mission of peace.

Seven years prior to the signing of the Lateran Accord,

Pius XI, who as usual was not invited to the Genoa Conference, wrote an open letter to the Archbishop of Genoa in which he suggested that the victors and vanquished should come together to settle their differences. Germany and Russia were both represented at Genoa and it was rumored that Tchitcherin would visit the Vatican after the Conference to thank the Holy See for the generous help given to the starving population of Russia. This rumor proved groundless and the contact that the Holy Father craved with Russia was not effected. In another letter to Cardinal Gasparri, Pius again extended an invitation to Russia. In fact, three separate overtures were made to contact the U. S. S. R. Remembering Pius' own personal experiences as Papal Nuncio in Poland and what he saw there when the Bolsheviks were at the gates, the attempts he made to enter Russia and his efforts to save the lives of his own religious Faithful and the Eastern Orthodox followers, it is not surprising that all these rebuffs should have resulted in his determination to exert every effort to first come to terms with Italy and then meet each problem in the foreign field within the framework of the Lateran Accord, never surrendering his prerogatives as spiritual leader to call political leaders to their responsibility to walk in the ways of God and to promote the peaceful collaboration of men of good-will.

Many—even Catholics in some quarters—have criticized Pius for surrendering too much authority when he signed the Accord with Italy and claim that he has made himself a vassal of the Italian Fascist State. No doubt he himself has had some searchings of heart. For we repeat what we said at the beginning of this biographical study that, although the Pope is infallible in regard to matters of dogma, when he speaks *ex cathedra;* he is not, nor does he claim to be, infallible in matters of policy and of judgment of mundane considerations. That he does not believe himself impervious to error in worldly matters is evidenced by the fact that he has revised his own earlier judgment on more than one occasion. It is also evident in the spirit of humility and caution breathing through all his writings. Nor do we base our thesis of the practical good that would ensue in the international field if the spiritual leadership of the Papacy were invoked on the belief that his leadership would be a fool-proof barricade against the greed and wickedness of men; but because, if men of good will have a vital passionate desire for world peace, they should ally themselves with spiritual forces. For the healing of the nations this reservoir of spiritual power should be tapped.

All the efforts of the last four Popes of the Catholic Church have been directed toward the religious pacification of the world. But the world has turned a deaf ear. The rulers of states have been more interested in the aggrandizement of their own power than in bringing about the peace and security and happiness of mankind. There is a formidable tradition of Christian experience behind the Holy See that admirably fits it to cope with problems that baffle the best lay minds. The fact that the Pope is the recognized head of four hundred million souls scattered all over the world invests him with a responsibility that could never betray their faith. Now that the temporal power of the Papacy is clearly defined and limited, the old bogey of Papal interference in the purely civic concerns of states is dispelled; and all men and women of good will whose ardent love of peace is more precious than their moth-eaten prejudices (the out-moded survivals of a society that believed in witchcraft) should welcome and, indeed, commandeer the intervention of this untried powerful agent for world peace. No puerile apprehensions should cloud the minds of men and women dedicated to the cause of peace. They might gladly join together to invoke the spiritual offices of such an experienced and well-equipped organization for dealing with international problems, and support the Holy See in its destined mission of world pacification.

To those who glibly blame Pope Pius XI for not castigating—even to the extent of excommunicating Mussolini—the Ethiopian adventure; first, in justice let us remind ourselves of the impassioned plea for peace addressed to the soldiers in San Paolo fuori le Mura prior to the embarkation of the troops for Africa. In words of sublime consecration, declaring he would be unworthy of his high responsibility as their Father and as Supreme Pontiff, if he did not renew his consecration to the cause of peace, he recapitulated all the fervor and logic of his pastoral encyclicals. This address was supressed by the press of Italy. On another occasion he warned and exhorted against wars of aggression and even against "wars of unjust defense." He never blessed the Italian army, although he did permit the chaplains to follow the soldiers—as was his and their obvious duty. That he did

not join in the chorus of condemnation of Italy and back
the fifty-four states of the League in their attempt to invoke "sanctions"—or in other words, a blockade to starve
out his own countrymen, does not indicate that he gave
his approval to the campaign. We find no inconsistency
here in the avowed champion of peace, and reserve the
right to question this method as the wisest and most
Christian for promoting conditions conducive to mutual
understanding to bring about an early settlement of the
conflict. To join in with such a campaign against the
people of a great nation for the sake of an appearance
of consistency would never be the Papal attitude. Such
slavish conformity to the appearance of consistency
would be a vice, common enough to governments which
indulge in "face saving" to hide a betrayal of principle.

We know now that Mussolini had this African ven-
ture in mind as far back as 1933, provided the League
did not hearken to Italy's "just demands" and give her
satisfaction without a resort to arms.

The Holy See did not create any of the conditions
that led up to the Great War and had no part in the
framing of the infamous Versailles Treaty. On the contrary, all the overtures of the pontiffs from the time of
Pius IX were rejected by jealous nationalistic powers.
Without exception they turned a deaf ear to the Vatican's appeals for peace—a peace founded upon justice
and the mutual rights of the contending parties, in the
spirit of that charity and mercy which Christ Himself
proclaimed. Yet, in spite of this consistent stupidly mo-
notonous policy of ignoring the Papal appeals, there are

those who innocently—or maliciously—ask: "Why didn't the Pope stop the Great War? He had the power." [6] Why didn't Pius XI stop the Ethiopian campaign? He had the weapon." Yes, he had the weapon—the weapon of excommunication. But, just as a labor leader has no moral right to call a strike unless he is sure that the cause is just and the outcome is reasonably certain, so the Pope would not be justified in wielding the weapon of excommunication unless, weighing the consequences of its application, he were assured that the good results would overbalance the evil. If Pius XI had resorted to the exercise of his undoubted prerogative, what should we have seen? In Italy, confusion worse confounded. All the blessings that have accrued because of a united people would have been jeopardized in civil war. And in the world—what? Who can say? We suspect the critics of Pius' "lack of action" of ungenerous motives to justify their own lack of honesty.

When we consider what obstacles have been placed in the way of every attempt to make a dent in the locked minds of the diplomats, and to contact responsible statesmen, what impassable barriers have been erected by selfish interests, we think it a marvel that so much has been begun in creating "a way of peace." Confronted with such obdurate stubbornness, it is amazing that the voice of the Pontiff of Rome continues to ring out in

---

[6] A misstatement. Benedict XV did not have the power, except theoretically. Only the bestowal of temporal power and the use of the radio and airplane have created the actual power for the Vatican to be heard over the prohibitions of censorship.

clarion tones to challenge and soften the hard hearts of men. It is a tribute to his sublime faith in ultimate goodness and his constancy of purpose in a holy cause.

.   .   .   .   .   .

We are still too close to Pius XI to do full justice to his remarkable pontificate. For sixteen years, if we view the labors of the Pope with impartial eyes, we see how persistent and very practical his efforts have been in the erection of an edifice for future pontiffs to enlarge and develop for the furtherance of his dream of *Pax Christi in Regno Christi*. Future, and we trust happier, generations will garner the fruits of his labors where another pontiff will reap what Pius XI has sown and watered; while a Voice will be heard echoing down the centuries: "Well done, good and faithful servant."

BIBLIOGRAPHY

Histories of Italy

Browning, Oscar; A Short History of Italy, P. Maglione & C. Strine, Rome, 1919

Gifford, Augusta Hale; Italy, Her People and Their Story from Romulus to Victor Emmanuel III, Lathrop Pub. Co., Boston, 1905

Gleichen, Lord Edward; Italy, Hodder and Stoughton, Ltd., London, 1923

Hunt, William; History of Italy, Macmillan & Co., London, 1885

Jamison, E. M., Ady, C. M., Vernon, K. D. & Sanford Terry, C.; Italy: Mediaeval and Modern, Clarendon Press, Oxford, 1919

Sedgwick, Henry Dwight; A Short History of Italy (476-1900), Houghton Mifflin & Co., Boston, 1905

Trevelyan, George Macaulay; Garibaldi and the Making of Italy, Longmans Green & Co., New York, 1911

Trevelyan, Mrs. Janet; A Short History of the Italian People from the Barbarian Invasions to the Attainment of Unity, Putnam, New York, 1926

Pope Pius XI

Canavan, Joseph E., S.J.; Pope Pius XI, Studies, Irish Quarterly Review, June, 1929, Vol. XVIII, No. 70

Fontenelle, Mgr. R.; His Holiness, Pope Pius XI, translated from the French by Rev. W. E. Brown; Burns Oates & Washbourne, London, 1923

Gasquet, Cardinal Francis Aidan; His Holiness, Pope Pius XI, A Pen Portrait, D. O'Connor, London, 1922

Gwynn, Dennis; Pius XI, The Holme Press, London, 1932

Novelli, Angelo, Rev.; *Pio XI* (*Achille Ratti*) MDCCCLVII-MCMXXII, Casa Editrice, "Pro Familia," Milan, 1923

Lombardo, P. T., Rev.; (translation of above into English) as *The Life of Pius XI*, Mt. Carmel Press, Yonkers, N. Y., 1925

Rushton, Gerald Wynne; *The Dynasty of Pius XI*, Burns Oates & Washbourne, Ltd., London, 1932

Townsend, W. & L.; *The Biography of His Holiness, Pope Pius XI*, Albert Marriott, Ltd., London, 1930

Williamson, Benedict; *The Story of Pope Pius XI*, P. J. Kenedy & Sons, New York, 1931

The Lateran Accord

Official Text of the Treaty between the Holy See and Italy, Nat. Cath. Welfare Conference, Washington, D. C., 1929

The Legal Position of the Holy See, by Mario Falco (Two lectures delivered in the University of Oxford and translated from the French by A. H. Campbell). Oxford University Press, London, 1935

Civis Romanus (pseud.); *The Pope Is King*, E. Benn, London, 1929

Mussolini

Fiori, Vittorio de; *Mussolini: The Man of Destiny*, Dutton, New York, 1928

Fortnightly Review; *The Origins of Fascism and the Evolution of Mussolini*, New York, 1924

Political Science Quarterly; vol. XLI, June, 1926, *Mussolini, Prophet of the Pragmatic Era in Politics*

Turati, Augusto; *A Revolution and Its Leader* (Introduction by Benedict Williamson & Foreword by Mussolini), Alexander-Ouseley, Ltd., London, 1930

Other Works Consulted

Eckhardt, Carl Conrad; *The Papacy and World Affairs*, University of Chicago Press, 1937

Huddleston, Sisley; *Those Europeans—Studies of Foreign Faces*, Putnam, New York, 1924

Ratti, Abate Achille (Pope Pius XI); *Climbs on Alpine Peaks,* T. Fisher Unwin, Ltd., Adelphi Terrace, London

Ratti, Rev. Achille (Pope Pius XI); *Essays in History* (1896-1912), London, 1934

Jubilaeum, Anno Santo, Religion, Marsano, G. B., Genoa

Seldes, George; *The Vatican; Yesterday, Today and Tomorrow,* (Historical chapters by George London & Ch. Pichon), Harpers, New York, 1934

Sherrill, Charles; *Great Personalities in the New Italy* (The King, Mussolini, the Pope and Cardinal Gasparri), Scribners, Oct. 1923, No. 4, Vol. LXXIV

Williams, Michael (in collaboration with Julia Kernan); *The Catholic Church In Action,* Macmillan, New York, 1934

Macaulay's *Essay on Ranke's "History of the Popes"*

Catholic Encyclopedia

Encyclopedia Britannica

Papal Documents

Rerum Novarum	Leo XIII
Praedecessoris Nostri	
Vacante Sede Apostolica	Pius X
Commissum Nobis	
Il Fermo Proposito	
Pacem Dei Mundus	Benedict XV
Ad Beatissimi	

Pius XI'S Addresses

To the Lenten Preachers of Rome
To the Diplomatic Corps
To the Students of Mondragone College
To the International Pilgrimage of Veterans of the World War
To the International Catholic Press Exhibition
To the Spanish Refugees

Pius XI'S Encyclicals

Caritate Christi Compulsi
Casti Connubii
Dilectissima Nobis

Divini Redemptoris
Iniquis Afflictisque
Mit Brennender Sorge
Non Abbiamo Bisogno
Nos Es Muy
Nova Impendit
Quadragesimo Anno
Rerum Ecclesiae
Rite Expiatis
Ubi Arcano Dei

The Encyclicals of Pius XI, James H. Ryan (of the faculty of
   Philosophy of the Catholic University of America, Wash.,
   D. C.), B. Herder Book Co., St. Louis, Mo.

INDEX OF PROPER NAMES